PRAISE FOR *INFLUENTIAL INTERNAL COMMUNICATION*

D1554802

'The book I wish I had when I was starting out in internal communication back in 2014: it would have accelerated my development and equipped me with perspectives on just how much great communication can have a transformative effect on organizations.

'Combining theory with practical quick tips, the book is a trusted companion to practitioners who truly desire to make a difference in their organizations. The sheer breadth of communication and business topics is impressive but written in a conversational tone that epitomizes Jenni's natural engaging style.

'Whether you are a newcomer to internal communication or a more seasoned practitioner, or you work in organisational design or human resources – Jenni Field's book is one that should sit on your desk.'
Krishan Lathigra, Interim Head of Internal Communication and Engagement, UK Department for Digital, Culture, Media and Sport

'An eclectic collection of valuable ideas and practical solutions for everyday internal communication challenges. This is a useful guide for practitioners who are interested in taking a broader perspective that incorporates understanding people and organizations.'
Dr Kevin Ruck, Co-founder, PR Academy

'This book is a practical guide that will not only equip communicators but inspire them too. It's packed with relevant theory and examples, that unlock the possibilities of effective internal communication. This book will help you have the right conversations, to drive everyone forward. I highly recommend it.'
Rachel Miller, Director, All Things IC

'A transformational book from a transformational and passionate professional. The Field Model is inspired and I can see it being utilized by organizations all over the world. There is no employee engagement without internal communications and this book will help you deliver both effectively.'
Matt Manners, Founder and CEO, Inspiring Workplaces Group

'An indispensable guide for leaders, communication professionals, students, and anyone interested in how to harness the power of communications to empower teamwork to make the dream work. In an increasingly virtual working environment, internal communication is the glue that bonds employee's view of reality and needs for purpose. Jenni Field reveals the Field Model with a practical guide on understanding, diagnosing, and fixing issues while guiding employee behaviour based on organizational priorities and strategies.'
Farzana Baduel, CEO, Curzon PR

'The book that we've waited for to leverage the perceived value gained for internal communication professionals during Covid-19 and help the discipline evolve officially from reactive and tactical to proactive and strategic. Jenni Field explains foundational concepts and provides an accessible model to help leaders and communication professionals alike solve real business problems with communication solutions.

'The key difference between external communication versus internal communication is focusing on the campaign versus the conversation. By sharing the Field Model, Jenni Field teaches you how to manage a series of conversations to understand, diagnose and fix business problems. She steers clear of the one-size-fits-all solutions and instead guides the reader on a journey to understand the challenges, symptoms perceptions before identifying potential solutions. The result is sure to create the long-term sustainable change leaders and organizations seek.'
Priya Bates, President, Inner Strength Communication

'In this book, Jenni Field reveals herself to be more than the leader at the front of the room advocating for the communication profession and its practitioners. In publishing the first comprehensive manual for internal communication for the pandemic/post-pandemic era, she reaches a new level of thought leadership in the field. This book raises tough questions for practitioners and their clients, while pursuing a disciplined agenda to align internal communication professionals to more effective and rigorous practices. Rather than making simple stuff complex, the author makes complex concepts simple and actionable, is unafraid to call out toxic practices and unyielding in her commitment to diagnosing challenges through research rather than executive opinion or personal intuition.'
Mike Klein, Principal, Changing The Terms and former EMENA Chair, IABC

'Jenni Field's model is business-performance focused, insightful and comprehensible. Leaders need to understand change dynamics and effectively engage with people; this book shows the way.'
David Stringer-Lamarre, Chair, IoD London Region and MD, Fortis Consulting London

'A book which should not only be read but, most of all, understood by all those working in internal communication. It demonstrates the power internal communication can have from a strategic perspective, not just channel and broadcast use.'
Ella Minty, Author, and Issues, Crisis and Reputation Lecturer and Adviser

Influential Internal Communication

Streamline your corporate
communication to drive efficiency
and engagement

Jenni Field

KoganPage

First published in Great Britain and the United States in 2021 by Kogan Page Limited

2nd Floor, 45 Gee Street	122 W 27th St, 10th Floor	4737/23 Ansari Road
London	New York, NY 10001	Daryaganj
EC1V 3RS	USA	New Delhi 110002
United Kingdom		India
www.koganpage.com		

Kogan Page books are printed on paper from sustainable forests.

ISBNs

Hardback	978 1 78966 615 1
Paperback	978 1 78966 613 7
Ebook	978 1 78966 614 4

British Library Cataloguing-in-Publication Data

A CIP record for this book is available from the British Library.

Library of Congress Cataloging-in-Publication Data

Names: Field, Jenni, author.
Title: Influential internal communication : steamline your corporate
  communication to drive efficiency and engagement / Jenni Field.
Description: 1 Edition. | New York : Kogan Page Inc, 2021. | Includes
  bibliographical references and index.
Identifiers: LCCN 2020057337 (print) | LCCN 2020057338 (ebook) | ISBN
  9781789666137 (paperback) | ISBN 9781789666151 (hardback) | ISBN
  9781789666144 (ebook)
Subjects: LCSH: Communication in management. | Communication in
  organizations. | Corporate culture. | Organizational effectiveness.
Classification: LCC HD30.3 .F54 2021 (print) | LCC HD30.3 (ebook) | DDC
  658.4/5–dc23
LC record available at https://lccn.loc.gov/2020057337
LC ebook record available at https://lccn.loc.gov/2020057338

Typeset by Hong Kong FIVE Workshop, Hong Kong
Print production managed by Jellyfish
Printed and bound by CPI Group (UK) Ltd, Croydon CR0 4YY

CONTENTS

ABOUT THE AUTHOR

Jenni Field has worked with organizations for over 16 years, helping them understand how internal communication can have real influence and impact on the everyday. She helps business leaders understand how to get their teams to work better – issues in their operations are diagnosed so they can work more efficiently, and the chaos is then fixed by implementing tactics that will give the desired results.

She created The Field Model to provide a framework for organisations to work through after setting up her own consultancy in 2017.

Jenni has been a leader in the communications industry for years. She has led research into communicating with deskless workers, co-founded The IC Crowd (a Twitter-based community for those working in internal communications) and in 2020 launched a podcast, Calm Edged Rebels, with her good friends and fellow consultants Trudy Lewis and Advita Patel.

Jenni has volunteered in the PR and Communications industry since 2012 with the Chartered Institute of Public Relations (CIPR) and in 2020 was the President, leading them through significant change in light of the Covid-19 pandemic.

She is a Chartered practitioner, a fellow of the CIPR and qualified in internal communication. She is also an accredited facilitator and an international speaker – you'll find her either on stage or speaking virtually about her research, how organizations can change when they understand the power of communication and more.

For this book, she has read, researched, interviewed and explored the business world through the eyes of a professional communicator. In her view, everything leads to communication so learning how to be effective and influential with internal communication is paramount to business success.

PRAISE FOR *JENNI FIELD*

'Brill start to the day with the inspirational Jenni Field. My takeaway: listen to understand where your leadership team is and re-frame when you need to so they get the value you're adding as a strategic function.'
Lee Leyshon, Assistant Director Engagement and Communications

'Jenni Field is our go-to facilitator for our events. She is a natural facilitator – confident, authoritative and highly engaging. In the planning phases, she brings independence and objectivity, challenging our thinking and guiding us towards better solutions.'
Katie Macaulay, Managing Director

'Jenni Field combines a breezy, accessible style with an encyclopaedic knowledge of the internal comms and engagement space. Never lost for words, she thinks ably on her feet.'
Marc Wright, Founder and Director

'Jenni Field has provided us with a great framework on how to communicate successfully and efficiently within our team. It's the simple things often overlooked that Jenni instils in us that help to direct the business into a successful place.'
Danny Meade, Personal Trainer

'If there is one person that makes me want to do more with my time it's the ever-inimitable Jenni Field.'
Annie Lordon, Communications Business Partner

'Jenni Field's insights have helped me get a clearer understanding of what techniques and approaches to use to get the desired outcomes. She will also ask challenging questions to get me thinking more about the situation too.'
Alex Whittingham, Communications Business Partner

ACKNOWLEDGEMENTS

Trudy Lewis and Advita Patel – thank you for being my constant champions and for helping me shape the outline of this book from the very beginning.

Chloe Michel – thank you for your time to help me with the case studies included in this book to help bring my thinking and examples to life.

Benjamin Ellis – thank you for the insight into diagnostics and data. A complex topic, and the conversations we had helped me make sense of the challenges we often face as communicators.

Introduction

This book will explore how to transform your organization using influential internal communication. Whether you work in communications or as a leader of an organization, understanding the power of communication will help you drive efficiency and engagement. This book will offer practical advice, grounded in theory and my own Field Model. The Field Model has been designed to allow organizations to diagnose what is really creating the chaos inside the organization, and how internal communication can create a sense of calm. I strongly believe that all challenges inside organizations can be fixed through a better understanding of communication and people.

This book outlines the fundamental skills and tools you need to bring calm to your organization.

As the world of work is impacted forever by Covid-19 and the use of technology has been embedded in organizations at pace, there is one person or one team who can help leaders make sense of it all – the internal communication team. If no such team exists in your organization, this book will help you gain the skills needed to put things in place to improve internal communication.

As we look closely at organizations later in the book we will explore the impact of lockdown as well as how globalization and technology play a role in how organizations work today and in the future.

During the Covid-19 pandemic in 2020, research carried out by the Institute of Internal Communication (IoIC, nd) suggested that practitioners believe they will benefit from the crisis, with 90 per cent believing the situation will have a 'very positive' (32 per cent) or 'positive' (58 per cent) impact on the internal communication profession.

This is a very positive outlook. Research over the last decade tells us that the barriers to internal communication and the challenges faced haven't changed much. There is hope that a global pandemic will help leaders understand the value and impact it can bring but that hope is not yet a certainty.

For many, the internal communication function is the place where you go to get a PowerPoint tidied up or a newsletter out to the organization. It is not always seen as the strategic function it can be, partnering with every department and every level in the organizational hierarchy. There is a strong need for good and appropriate channels inside organizations to ensure the flow of information and news but this isn't all it is. This is where we will start in Chapter 1. Making sure we are all aligned on what internal communication is and how it can support organizations.

Part One of this book explores internal communication and chaos. We have to start by grounding ourselves in the role of internal communication – what it means, how it works and where it adds value. Internal communication might not have been around for as long as some other core business functions like HR and marketing, but it is needed in organizations today more than ever. We will explore the role of chaos in organizations – how the patterns behind the apparent confusion can lead to calm in the workplace.

We will go on to explore people and organizations – content that is fundamental to the success of an internal communication function. In work we can focus on commercials, bottom line and productivity but with that focus we have lost sight of the human side of work. For internal communication to be truly influential, there has to be a basic understanding of people.

In Part Two we will explore the Field Model, and how diagnosing what's truly wrong in an organization will lead to communication solutions that you and your team can implement to lead the company to calm.

The theory behind the Field Model is that good communication can take an organization from chaos to calm. To be able to do this we need to understand people and organizations better. They have changed over the decades of work, and the need to adapt as managers and leaders shouldn't be underestimated. In addition, we have become stuck in a world of 'constant change', which is why we have to explore chaos in more detail and what it means for the workplace.

We have been through several revolutions, and the technology revolution has impacted organizations and their ability to operate globally, and at pace, more than any other. I'd argue that constant change isn't a real concept and that this is, in fact, chaos. Chaos where balance and order can be introduced through understanding people and organizations more.

This isn't a book about theory – it is packed with references and theories that support the models and concepts but there has to be practical advice that can be applied immediately. The Field Model is designed to do exactly that – diagnose what's going on and provide practical advice to resolve the challenges in the form of listening, discussing and navigating conflict.

The Field Model

The model has three parts: Understand, Diagnose and Fix. I have watched organizations jump from 'understand' to 'fix' without diagnosing the reason. This often ends in more hard work and difficult conversations because no time has been spent diagnosing why things are happening. This approach means you're just treating the symptoms, not the root cause.

It is easy to understand something is wrong, bring in someone to help deliver training or a campaign to fix it. But most of the time this is a short-term fix, which turns into a longer-term expense of time and money.

Sometimes I will hear people say 'we already know this', but they only know the problem. They understand people aren't happy, but they haven't explored why. They haven't been able to diagnose why this is and they haven't looked at themselves as part of the problem. This is one of the biggest challenges for leadership teams. And when it comes to looking at communication inside organizations we have to look at individual style and impact. This can be uncomfortable but the long-term impact of not having some short-term discomfort can result in commercial losses and a direct link to customer satisfaction.

When you're trying to understand what's happening inside organizations you need to ask questions like this:

- What made you pick up the phone?
- How long has your leadership team been in place?
- Where are your employees?
- How do you talk to everyone?
- Do you have any data about how employees feel about work?
- What are the core performance measures for the organization?
- Why do you think there is a problem?

And when you want to diagnose what's going on you need to choose the right tool for the job – from listening interviews to surveys, there are different tools for different reasons. We will explore them all so you can identify which one is right for your organization, and as we come to explore how you fix these issues with communication, we help you identify the right ones for the problems you're having.

The fix is the plan. The plan is always different because every organization is different. The structure, the ownership, the culture, the purpose – they are always different. There are some themes that tend to be common, which you can see here, but there will always be specific areas of focus for the organization:

- upskilling the team or individual;
- leadership communication/behaviour changes;
- consistency and commitment;
- culture;
- respect;
- prioritization;
- organizational structure.

I will always say that the fix will require an investment of time, a shift in focus to the difficult aspects of organizations that require thought and attention. It is time and focus that have to change, not necessarily the financial investment. If your organization works at pace (and we will talk about what that looks like later in the book) then is that pace focused and is it ensuring that everyone remains engaged?

In the final chapter we will outline the ways you can fix things based on specific problems – the problems or the chaos that we have

Table 0.1 Example of application of the Field Model in Chapter 8

Understand the chaos	Diagnostic tool	Diagnostic themes to explore	The fix	Timescale – team size dependent
People aren't getting along in the same team and it's causing issues for everyone	Listening interviews with individuals and peers	Relationships across the team generally Relationship of the team to the leader Understanding of team purpose Individual purpose	SDI could be recommended to better understand strengths and anchors Coaching conversations with individuals and teams	1–6 months
Team A and Team B don't work well together, and we need them to	Listening interviews (plus a survey, depending on size of team)	Why the teams need to work together What's the benefit of them working well together? Role of the leaders in each team and their relationship	Process for the task to be completed to be reviewed Leader relationship coached through to working better together	3–9 months

seen before. You'll find tables that outline the way to diagnose the issue, what to look out for in the themes and the fix, as well as a timescale (but with the caveat that this depends on the size of the organization or team).

Table 0.1 is an example of what you can find in the final chapter.

There is a lot covered in the following chapters and you'll find that it draws on insight and research from across the globe, from experts in neuroscience, vulnerability, motivation, chaos and data. The workplace is a complex place. We have had years of working in different ways and with the expansion of knowledge work over manual labour, we need to adapt how we think about connecting those people who work there.

This is not always a comfortable read. There are often things that have been swept under the carpet because they are too hard or too uncomfortable. Here we delve right into those and explore beneath the surface of what you can do to adapt and change things to improve the communication inside your organization.

Reference

IoIC (nd) IoIC Covid-19 survey: trust, influence and cutting through the noise, www.ioic.org.uk/industry-news/ioic-covid-19-survey-effective-messaging-is-building-trust (archived at https://perma.cc/KQ7K-QU3W)

PART ONE
Foundations

Introduction to internal communication

01

Communication inside organizations, between employees, is internal communication. It's often part of PR due to its link to relationships and it can also be linked to HR, due to the core component being employees.

Communicating with employees is not the same as communicating with other stakeholders. Employees have a different relationship with the organization from customers, they are part of it, and they belong to it.

To define internal communication is challenging. There are hundreds of definitions because the breadth of what it includes is huge. Over the years, there have been several definitions from academics, authors, consultants and those working in-house as an internal communications manager, head of or director of internal communications.

My definition of internal communication is:

> Internal communication includes everything that gets said and shared inside
> an organization. As a function, its role is to curate, enable and advise on best
> practice for organizations to communicate effectively, efficiently and in an
> engaging way.

The Institute of Internal Communication (IoIC) says:

> At the most basic level, you have to communicate well at the right time so
> employees know what is expected of them and what is happening in the
> organization. At a deeper level, for employees to feel engaged with their
> workplace and give their best, they have to see that their organization cares

about their views and understand how their role contributes towards overall business objectives (IoIC, ndb).

For many people working as an internal communications manager, director or business partner, there is a need to define the role of internal communication inside the organization they work for.

In some organizations there is a whole department for internal communication. In others, it is a bolt-on to the PA for the CEO. It is this variety that makes it increasingly challenging for internal communicators to make headway in elevating its role to the strategic function it can be. It is also what contributes to different expectations from different leadership teams, which make it hard to identify the right skills, structure and outcomes needed for the function.

The IoIC outlines five reasons why internal communication is important today:

1 **Economic climate** – lifelong job security is now a rarity, and so the former social contract of unquestioning loyalty (from the employee) for job security (from the employer) has been broken. This means organizations have to work harder on relationships with their people.

2 **Importance of delivering great customer experience** – organizations have realized that a disconnect can quickly occur between the promises of promotional activity and what is actually experienced by customers if employees are not clear about what they are supposed to be doing or completely behind it.

3 **More democratic/consultative** – organizations have become less hierarchical and bureaucratic. People do not just want to be told things – they expect involvement and dialogue.

4 **New technology** – the ways in which communication takes place, and the forms that are now accepted and expected, cannot be 'controlled' in the same way as previous methods could.

5 **Frequent change** – organizations have to keep modifying how they operate to remain competitive. It is more challenging to keep employees motivated and moving in the right direction in these circumstances.

With these five points to consider, it's easy to see why internal communication needs more focus from leadership to help organizations thrive. The factors outlined here are only being accelerated in light of the Covid-19 pandemic. Its link to customer experience and employee experience is closer than ever. It is vital to the introduction of technology in the pandemic-accelerated organizational change as workforces around the world were locked down in their homes.

In times of crisis, the need for good internal communication is often a focus. The sometimes under-resourced function is now the one that is needed most to help keep the organization going, as people need access to information and technology to do their jobs effectively.

It's too early to identify the long-term impact of Covid-19 on internal communication but there is hope in the community that the understanding of the need for human connection at work will change things. There is now a recognition that flexibility in the workplace is key for society today, and that for knowledge workers (those who are office based), work can be done anywhere you have a computer. The world of work will be changed forever, and the internal communication function is central to that being a success.

Professional bodies

For years there have been conversations around the need for internal communication to have a seat at the board table, and how it deserves more recognition from business leaders than it currently receives.

To provide a comparison, looking at the link between functions in organizations and professional bodies can give some indication where the issues lie for those in internal communication.

HR (human resources) as we know it today used to be called the personnel function. The Chartered Institute of Personnel and Development (CIPD) started in 1913 as the Welfare Workers' Association (WWA). They were granted a Royal Charter in 2000 and are known as the professional body for HR and people development.

The finance function – often the core of an organization – had a similar time frame as a Chartered body. The Chartered Institute of Management Accountants (CIMA) was founded in 1919.

The final body to mention is the Chartered Institute of Marketing (CIM), which was founded in 1911.

You can see the time it has taken for these professions to become more standard and more recognized. When we look at the professional bodies linked to internal communication, and more broadly PR, then you can see that the role of communication in business had not been seen as a professional practice until 1938 at the earliest. There is an assumption here that the formation of a professional body signals a change for that profession; even without that assumption we can see that the role of internal communication inside organizations might not have the same weight as some of these other functions, simply because it has not had time to develop the recognition it needs.

- The Institute of Internal Communication (IoIC) was created in 1949 and was then known as the British Association of Industrial Editors (BAIE). In 1995 it rebranded to CIB: Communicators in Business and in 2010 it became the IoIC that we know today.

- The Chartered Institute of Public Relations (CIPR) was originally known as the Institute for Public Relations when it was founded in 1948. It was awarded Chartered status in 2005.

- The Public Relations Consultants Association was founded in 1969. It changed its name in 2016 to become the Public Relations and Communications Association.

- The International Association of Business Communicators (IABC) was originally known as the American Association of Industrial Editors (AAIE), which was founded in 1938. In 1970 IABC was formed as we know it today, following a merger between AAIE and the International Council of Industrial Editors (ICIE). Corporate Communicators Canada merged with IABC in 1974, expanding its membership.

Figure 1.1 IoIC profession map 2020

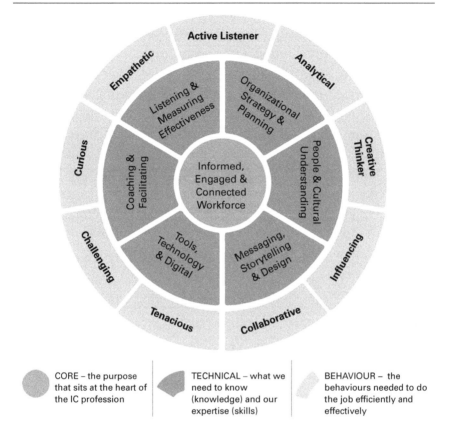

Active Listener

Empathetic

Analytical

Listening & Measuring Effectiveness

Organizational Strategy & Planning

Curious

Creative Thinker

Coaching & Facilitating

Informed, Engaged & Connected Workforce

People & Cultural Understanding

Challenging

Tools, Technology & Digital

Messaging, Storytelling & Design

Influencing

Tenacious

Collaborative

CORE – the purpose that sits at the heart of the IC profession

TECHNICAL – what we need to know (knowledge) and our expertise (skills)

BEHAVIOUR – the behaviours needed to do the job efficiently and effectively

This links to investment in the function by organization leaders, as well as the skills of the internal communicator. The skills needed to be successful in internal communication have adapted over the years, and in 2020 The Institute of Internal Communication updated its profession map to reflect the behaviours and skills needed today (Figure 1.1).

The list of behaviours here could apply to many functions inside organizations but the importance of empathy, listening and tenacity should not be underestimated for the internal communicator. These are core skills when it comes to relationship building, and for internal communication to succeed in influencing, there have to be these 'human' skills at the core.

Eight golden rules

In 2014 the eight golden rules from Fitzpatrick and Valskov were outlined in their book *Internal Communications: A manual for practitioners*. These rules are still very relevant for the communication professional and function today, and you can see the link between people, organizations and communication even then (Figure 1.2).

These rules may seem simple but combining them to support organizations is the art of internal communication. The currency of PR and communication is in ethics, leadership and strategy; communication with employees requires all three.

Rule 2 is one that many internal communication functions struggle with today. The importance of business acumen for those working in communications has been on the skills list for many years. The Chartered Institute of Public Relations State of the Profession survey

Figure 1.2   Eight golden rules

Rule 1	• It's about results and outcomes, not activity – ask the question 'what do we want people to do?'
Rule 2	• It's about the business – there has to be a link to the needs of the business. Without it, we are not adding any value
Rule 3	• We don't drive with our eyes shut – know your audience. You cannot do that from behind a desk either!
Rule 4	• People have two ears and one mouth, and so should organizations – listen. Communication is not one-way
Rule 5	• Come with data, leave with respect – gather data and use evidence. It's needed for your own credibility and to enable sound decisions
Rule 6	• Line managers matter – they hold the key to many challenges inside organizations
Rule 7	• There is no silver bullet – technology is not going to solve the communication challenges inside your organization
Rule 8	• What we do matters – internal communicators are in a privileged role and can have huge impact on individual employees' lives

shows that it has been a skills gap since 2017. The reasons for business acumen not being addressed seemed to link to time and the focus on tasks to complete. These rules were written in 2014 – the skills gaps have remained through to 2017 and beyond. It would great to see business acumen off the list in future as communicators take the time to understand organizations, the financials that are so important to success and the way things work. This is why these golden rules remain very relevant and very true today. They may be seven years old but the rules of the internal communication game are still the same.

The challenges for internal communication have continued for decades. It has to be influential to be effective, and it has to impact on the people who work for the organization and the way the organization operates. If it doesn't, it's not having any business impact.

The value and impact of internal communication on organizations

In 2017 the Chartered Institute of Public Relations' (CIPR) internal communication group carried out research into the value and impact of internal communication. They interviewed CEOs to find out exactly what they thought:

- Internal communication is important, but as it doesn't generate profit as a function, it was never going to be placed above the ones that do in terms of value to the organization.
- Culture came up as an area that was impacted by internal communication, as well as engagement – in some cases internal communication functions were seen as the 'owners' of culture.
- 'Employee engagement' and 'internal communication' are used interchangeably by internal communicators.
- There is a lack of alignment between internal communication teams and management.
- Internal communication teams are the custodians of translating strategy, company values and priorities.

- There was a strong consensus that measuring increased productivity and improved performance as a result of internal communications was difficult.

Looking at internal communication through the lens of a CEO helps bring some reality to the role. Many departments inside organizations get stuck trying to demonstrate worth and value, internal communicators more so than others, based on the small budgets often allocated to the work.

Determining what value means for the leader in your organization is important. Have the conversation and if you are a leader, ask yourself what value looks like to you. It will be different from person to person. For some it's about managing risk, for others it's about engaging the front line to deliver great customer service. It's a conversation that has to be had for internal communication functions to have any influence inside the organization.

This links to the need to define internal communication inside the organization. Some definitions were shared earlier in the book but as they can be so broad, creating your own for your organization is really important. The definition of it should come from conversations with leadership and discussions about how it supports the organizational objectives. This has to be the starting point for any function to ensure that the focus is in the right place and the output is effective.

Communication theory – underpinning internal communication

The practice of internal communication is grounded in communication theory. For many, the academic side of communication is unknown, but you can become qualified, chartered and complete a master's in internal communication – just like you can for other professions that operate in organizations today.

The theory is important because internal communication is not just about opinion. When there is research and academic study to support it, leaders find it easier to understand why things should be done a certain way and what the impact of improved internal communication would be for their organization. I completed my qualification in internal communication when I was told my opinion was not enough in the boardroom. While this felt unjust at the time, completing the qualification meant I could test my own knowledge against theory and have the weight of academia behind me.

Having a qualification helps you position a business case better. It brings an external perspective to what you're doing because you have networked with others outside of your organization. It can help you ensure that you have a way of working that looks at stakeholders, models of communication, culture, channels and more.

Foundations

As you go further into this book, you'll read more about organizations and people. Internal communication is the glue that holds an organization together and as such there is a need to understand organizations and people in some depth.

As we explore more about what this means for internal communication, there are six foundations for impactful communication that support the rules we have already covered:

1 **Focus on the audience**: Develop a true understanding of your target audience. This isn't about you, it's about them. What you think works might not be what is right for your audience – you need them to be at the front of your mind at all times. Get to know them: what are the different stakeholder groups in your part of the business? What do they do every day, how do they work?

2 **Set a clear goal**: Always be clear about why you are doing what you are doing. What are you trying to achieve? Do you want them to be informed? Do you want them to do something differently?

3 **Get the tone right**: While studies suggest there is a split between tone, body language and words, this lacks verification. Each component part of communication has a role to play and tone, in a world where email dominates, is something we often miss or assume. Drop the jargon, explain each acronym and be mindful

that internally there can be a language understood only by those around you.

4 Keep it simple: Studies have found that people think you're less intelligent and less credible if you use long words when shorter words will do. Remember, the power of silence in difficult conversations allows you to keep things simple – don't over-qualify a decision.

5 Structure to make your point: Be logical – think about the flow that would make sense to the audience – think about a film/tv series or a supermarket flow. There should be no surprises – remember that structure can take place over a longer period, so telling people there is no pay rise shouldn't come as a complete surprise, as the message should have been signalled throughout the year. Think about the point you're going to make: tell them what you're going to tell them, tell them and then tell them what you told them.

6 Adapt to the medium: Medium/channel are important – they contribute to the message. You wouldn't text someone to sack them because using that channel makes the message worse. Don't get stuck in the same channel, eg PowerPoint/meeting. Remember the other foundations – does that channel work for the audience, does it support your goal?

There is a lot of theory that can be explored for communicators, but this book isn't about the academic side of what we do. It's about providing practical advice to help you shift the organization by creating influential and effective communication strategies that have an impact.

The six foundations outlined above are enough to help you consider your own style of communication. Focus on your audience, have clear structure and purpose, and that alone will make a difference to the way things work inside the organization.

The role of communication inside organizations is paramount to success. This isn't necessarily new information, but the lack of planning, strategy, or consideration of content and channels is where things can start to fall down.

Communication channels

A communication channel is the mechanism you use to communicate. In addition to internal communication this could be a text message, a letter or an email (to name a few).

There are lots of channels available both inside and outside organizations. The rise of social media, smartphones and apps has meant there has been a shift in how we communicate with employees.

The first formal employee publications can be dated back to 1840 and organizations today continue to use magazines as a channel to communicate with employees. Internal communicators now have a range of tools: from video to printed newsletters, as well as online collaboration platforms (Office 365/SharePoint), podcasts, chatbots – the list goes on.

In the last 15 years alone the shift from print to digital has been exponential as organizations shift to working globally and remotely. This doesn't mean that internal digital communication is the solution to all problems – far from it – nor does it mean that all organizations are embracing technology and investing in it – they aren't. What it does mean is that the purpose of the communication channel and the skills of the communicator have shifted.

The channels are no longer purely broadcast. Before the introduction of technology, the ability to listen to employees was limited, and due to some management theories, it was actively discouraged. Today in society, organizations aren't able to push messages out to any stakeholder group and walk away. People want conversation, discussion, dialogue. And for employees, they want to be part of decisions and be heard more than any other group.

The audience/employees are now able to participate in creating the content. The need to curate that content and share it to encourage conversation is different from writing up an interview and publishing it in a magazine. The skills needed to create and edit a magazine are not the same as the skills needed to design the architecture for a digital collaboration platform.

As internal communicators, our skills have to adapt in line with the pace of technology and organizational change. Leaders are asking more of internal communicators today – more in terms of their knowledge around which channel to use in a sea of options but also around advice and expertise that ensure that channel is going to engage and influence the audience.

The list of channels can go on and on. Gallagher's Employee Experience and Communication division list the following channels in their annual State of the Sector research (Gatehouse, 2020), which provides some helpful context about the options available:

- conferences;
- roadshows;
- town halls;
- informal get-togethers;
- team meetings run by line managers;
- web calls/conference calls;
- lunch and learn;
- employee forums;
- communication champions;
- employee magazines;
- printed newsletters;
- letters;
- desk drops;
- posters;
- flyers;
- brochures;
- mobile messaging;
- video;
- email announcements;
- apps;
- e-newsletters;
- internal social channels;
- digital signage;
- intranet;
- AI;
- blogs;
- extranet;
- podcasts.

The mix of channels used for every organization will be different. Factors like locations, operational model, leadership and culture all play a role in determining the right mix. Advice is usually to have a mix of print, digital and face to face, and to ensure there are channels that bring the voice of the employee into the centre to ensure there is two-way conversation.

You can map the channels in your organization on to a channel matrix – it helps to see the mix of what exists, where the gaps might be and also where there might be too many channels – and therefore too much noise – as well (Table 1.1).

Table 1.1 Example of a channel matrix table

Channel name	Method	Content	Frequency	Audience
eg The Bulletin	PDF document emailed to all colleagues	News from across the business linked to strategy and people news	Monthly	Internal only and all colleagues

Culture and communication

Communication helps to reinforce a company culture. Culture can have many definitions but ultimately, it is the way things get done inside the organization. How you communicate with each other is a tangible way of demonstrating that culture (Figure 1.3).

The culture will be seen through the channels used, the innovation of those channels (AI vs print), the tone of voice that is used to communicate with employees, the role of the employees in communication across the organization and more – it all signals the culture.

There are building blocks to culture – and as we work through the book, you'll see that culture and communication are constantly entwined. If culture is where the purpose, values and behaviours sit, then articulating those for employees and sharing stories that link to them is communication.

The alignment between behaviours and purpose is an important part of culture. How do things get done and does that match the purpose/values of the organization? The way you structure meetings, the expectations of timescales for delivery – they all play a role in signalling what it is like to work somewhere.

Figure 1.3   How culture is seen through communication

Culture is also closely linked to the employee experience. How people are treated throughout their life cycle within an organization is demonstrative of the culture. The challenge for organizations today is that they are often global. Culture therefore is a tricky one, as most organizations have a culture that is made up of 'macro cultures, nations and occupation' according to Edgar Schein (Moore, 2011).

As culture is built by humans and changed by humans, it's no surprise that things change over time. A global crisis will impact culture, much as a change in leadership or organization-wide changes in technology do – they will all have an impact on how things get done and how people work together.

A crisis like Covid-19 will impact culture. It will impact the rhythm of the organization. The rhythm of the organization is the way it operates. The meetings, the way things get done, the culture, the processes – all of it will have been impacted by Covid-19 because so much of the 'normal' way of work was disrupted. It is a topic that I discussed in detail throughout the crisis because it's important to explore what needs to change longer term, what has worked and what hasn't and what it has shown us about the culture of where we work. In order to get things done during the crisis, things had to change. There were shortages of products on shelves due to demand and supply challenges as well as a global shift for knowledge workers, who all became home-based. Looking at the rhythm of it all is important in order to know what needs to happen next.

As a communicator and as a leader, these are things you need to explore as you think about how people are connected and how they work together without the confines of an office space. It's an opportunity for us all to explore how the organization's drumbeat really should sound.

Change will always create a shift in the organization, and since the pandemic, we have had to consider new ways to use digital tools, the need to adapt to communicating in a purely virtual world, and the fact that the role of the communicator is now more in the spotlight than ever before.

The communicator looking at their culture needs to listen and explore how people feel. When there is huge change, and moving parts that lead to an inability to craft messaging, focus on how you want people to feel and work back from there.

Stop focusing on what to say and focus on how you want people to feel after they have been listened to. It will help you think differently and focus on the impact you are having.

Focusing on how people feel allows us to move away from a sense of panic and chaos. It allows us to put ourselves in the place of advising leadership. We are focusing their minds on the people and allowing empathy to lead.

Flexible working and a change in the need to be in an office all the time has been a campaign for many years from various groups. We need better technology to allow hybrid teams to engage and communicate, and all of this will impact the culture of the organization.

The culture has to demonstrate why you do what you do, reflect your values and beliefs. Your behaviours must support what you stand for. All of this will shift in times of a global crisis like Covid-19 and there must be time to reflect and adapt as a communication function to support that.

As cultures shift, so does the power. The world of work has shifted from a top-down, autocratic way of working to networked, democratic and bottom-up. The CEO is no longer seen as the expert on what's needed on the front line and the voice of those serving customers can be listened to immediately with the use of technology.

The different skills of the communicator needed to adapt to all of this shouldn't be underestimated. In turn, the value they bring to the organization should also be recognized.

The difference between internal communication and employee engagement

Over the years there has been a lot of discussion around employee engagement, employee experience and internal communication. Traditional communication agencies have rebranded as employee engagement, and more recently as employee experience specialists, and the link to HR has grown.

Even though there is a difference between these three things, the research from CIPR in 2017 highlights that the three terms are used interchangeably. While the research interviewed CEOs about value it also interviewed internal communication practitioners about the role they play inside organizations.

In the verbatim comments, many of the respondents used a variety of these terms when talking about internal communication. And this is dangerous. It's dangerous because some of these terms are not used by leaders in business and if those working in the profession use different terms for the same thing it will lead to confusion – which won't help the strategic focus internal communicators can and should have.

There are distinct definitions – even if we have to pick just one from the list of internal communication:

Employee engagement: 'A workplace approach designed to ensure that employees are committed to their organization's goals and values, motivated to contribute to organizational success and are able at the same time to enhance their own sense of well-being' (Macleod and Clarke, 2009).

Internal communication: 'Everything that gets said and shared inside of an organization. As a function, its role is to curate, enable, and advise on best practice for organizations to communicate effectively, efficiently and in an engaging way' (Field, 2017).

Employee experience: 'Creating an operating environment that inspires your people to do great things' (Maylett and Wride, 2017) or, according to Jacob Morgan (2016), 'Designing an organization where people want to show up by focusing on the cultural, technological, and physical environments.'

Understandably, the employee experience and engagement definitions focus more on the individual and their well-being than on communication. They are also not just about communication – which is why the three terms need to be distinguished from each other and organizations need to understand the differences.

All three are intrinsically linked, but internal communication also needs to fulfil its basic purpose of communicating with those in the organization before it can embark on the winning of hearts and minds. The winning of hearts and minds is not solely down to communication. There are many factors that contribute – line manager relationships, fair pay, equal opportunities – to name a few.

Employee engagement is a core principle for internal communication and is based on the premise that people who feel so much for an organization and its ambitions will go above and beyond their job description.

Macleod and Clarke's 'Engaging for Success: enhancing performance through employee engagement' report (Macleod and Clarke, 2009) shows strong links to bottom line and productivity when companies dedicate resource to ensure employees are engaged. They claim there are four main enablers to employee engagement:

1 A strong strategic narrative.
2 Engaging managers who focus their people and treat them as individuals.
3 Providing employees with a voice throughout the organization for reinforcing and challenging views.
4 Ensuring there is organizational integrity – the values are implicit, not just wallpaper.

In my experience, these four enablers are not of equal weight. I believe that the way you measure engagement is key to these being linked to productivity. I also believe that you can have some of these and not others and still see 'engagement' inside the organization.

For example, I have experience working in organizations where the narrative was strong – it might not have been particularly purposeful, but everyone knew why they were doing what they were doing. This led to great performance and engagement in terms of delivery and desire to get the job done but all other enablers were missing. In other places, there has been no strategic narrative but a strong sense of providing employees with a voice – this led to a revolving door of employees leaving and joining.

What is important here is that we look at all the aspects around internal communication and employee engagement together. They aren't the same thing but they are linked. The four enablers provide a great framework for organizations to draw from but having all four working in tandem at the same time with a great communication strategy and plan being executed is rare. Don't be set up for failure.

These enablers are a good foundation – but there is more complexity to engagement, and it needs more research into how it is measured, as well as how it links to internal communication, before it can be summarized so quickly. Engagement and communication do go together but the definitions we have explored here show how they are different; engagement is almost an output as a result of internal communication.

A model for internal communication strategy and planning

This model for creating an influential internal communication strategy and plan has been created to ensure the output is aligned to data (Table 1.2). It has been used in every organization I have worked in to set up the communication function. Each step has to be completed; they don't need to follow each other as some can be done together, but it's important to work through the whole process.

There are five steps to the model, and it starts with insight. We cannot make decisions about the right way to communicate inside an organization without data. If we try, then the decision is based on assumption and opinion, which is dangerous and easily disputed when it comes to budget setting. Later in the book we will spend time looking at data in detail – how to gather insight and the different tools you can use to 'diagnose' what's going on inside the organization.

The Field Model was created on the back of this model for communication strategy and planning:

Table 1.2   A model for an internal communications plan and strategy

Phase	Overview	Summary
Insight	Look at any existing research into employee engagement/internal communication and also any research with customers or other stakeholders Run surveys that cover employee effectiveness and engagement, communications audits and/or culture trackers Explore the use of focus groups, interviews over the phone to verify and explore the data	• Culture research • Perception internally and externally • Primary or secondary research
Business intelligence	Review all the material that exists that talks about the organization – annual report, case studies, marketing material, etc Look at the flow of communication across the organization to understand how the business works – who needs to talk to who and how you provide the services you do to your customers	• Business process • What does the organization do? • IT infrastructure

Table 1.2 *continued*

Phase	Overview	Summary
Principles	Create a set of guiding principles for the communication function and strategy. This will set out what is needed to resource the activity and whether there needs to be a plan to recruit anyone into the team. The principles should be aligned to the business strategy	• Function objectives • Principles for the organization • Alignment of business strategy and communications strategy
Communication	This is the creation of the communication strategy It should include any development needs for the leadership team or line managers and any workshops that might be needed It will include a content strategy and a channel matrix with a clear plan for the year.	• Channel matrix • Audience mapping • Content strategy • Information matrix
Measurement	The principles agreed enable the measurement as there will be clear objectives for success. The insight phase provides the benchmark so improvements can be made. There should also be a measure against business performance and outcomes	• KPIs for success aligned to principles • Culture of active listening • Agreed to timescales

This strategy and planning model needs to be combined with a look at stakeholders, or audience. For internal communicators there is often complexity in the stakeholders as organizations might employ contractors, freelancers, people who are self-employed, and more. It is important to spend some time mapping the stakeholders of the organization. The best way to do this is to look at who has high or low influence and who has high or low impact. As an example, sometimes the personal assistants to the senior team have a high level of influence in the organization but they don't have a huge impact on decision making. Identifying those people who you need to engage with and who the stakeholders are that you need to consider is an important part for internal communications – especially as relationships internal to the organization are so important.

To group stakeholders you can look at:

- role;
- location;
- demographics, like age;
- department;
- online or deskless.

You can always add more categories, but this is a good starting point for you to think about.

Following the steps in the model will mean that the communication strategy and plan is aligned to the business strategy. This is the only way to ensure the internal communication is influential and that it will have an impact across the organization. It's easy to create noise inside an organization and set up channels to allow people to communicate with each other. But if this isn't thought through, with choices made based on data and insight, it can be increasingly challenging to measure and get senior buy-in for the long term.

If we go back to the rules we covered at the start of this chapter, you can see how the model reflects some of those principles. The principles or rules for internal communication haven't changed over the years. The tools used to communicate inside organizations have but the foundations have remained fairly constant.

Internal communication is something every organization has. Whether there is someone managing it, looking at it strategically, or there is just a rumour mill doing the work for you, it exists. If you haven't invested in it or explored how it can help you make the organization more efficient, then this chapter should help explain why it is important and how to make a start.

Continuing to ignore the value it can bring will only result in more chaos and more time and money wasted on trying to solve issues that can be fixed with better communication infrastructure and skills.

Where internal communication sits in the organization

In 2020 Gallagher's Employee Experience and Communication division published their 11th annual State of the Sector report (Gatehouse, 2020). This report is an industry look at the trends across the internal communication industry. From barriers to priorities and channels to team size, it covers a lot of ground to help communicators spot trends that will help with conversations and strategies in the year ahead. It also asks people where they sit inside organizations – HR or PR.

For many years there has been a debate about where internal communication should sit inside the organization. Should it report to HR, marketing, the CEO, corporate communications? The list can go on because it is a function that links so much of the organization together.

Does it even matter? As long as the function is working across the whole organization, where it sits in an organizational chart shouldn't necessarily be a focus, but for many it is. And for many, it is a conversation that champions the function sitting in HR. This makes sense when you consider that the main focus is employees. The role of internal communication is also linked to reputation and that suggests that it would also make sense for the role to sit within the corporate communications or PR function.

Figure 1.4 shows that for the majority, internal communication sits in the PR/corporate communication/corporate affairs function inside organizations.

While employees are the main focus, with technology and reputation so closely aligned, the home of internal communication should be the corporate communication function. The CIPR (nd) definition of PR is 'the planned and sustained effort to establish and maintain goodwill and mutual understanding between an organization and its publics.' 'Its publics' is important because this isn't the general public. Publics include anyone that has a link to an organization – and one of the most important stakeholders has to be its employees. In addition, when it comes to managing reputation (for which PR is

Figure 1.4 Data from State of the Sector showing where internal communication sits inside an organization

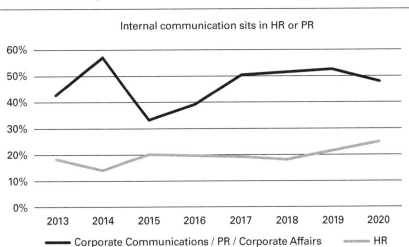

also responsible), the reputation of the organization/brand with employees is more and more important with the pace of society today.

The link to reputation might seem odd but as technology moves at pace, conversations that were once only in the canteen or only through an internal system can now be found on social media or leaked to the media. Over the years there have been several stories of internal memos from leadership teams shared with the press, and the gap between what you say your brand stands for and the reality of how you treat your employees is now front and centre for any member of the public to see.

Key points in this chapter

1 Internal communication doesn't have one definition. For your organization, define what the function will do and what internal communication is. This is important because it means you are setting the strategy for how internal communication can support the organizational objectives.

2 I define internal communication as everything that gets said and shared inside an organization. As a function, its role is to curate,

enable and advise on best practice for organizations to communicate effectively, efficiently and in an engaging way.

3 The Institute of Internal Communication (IoIC) suggests internal communication is important for organizations because of economic climate, customer experience, more democratic structures, new technology and frequent change.

4 The professional bodies linked to communication weren't founded until around 1938, in comparison to bodies for other core business functions, which started as early as 1911.

5 Rules for internal communication suggested in 2014 are still relevant today – the profession and the fundamental elements of it haven't changed.

6 To ensure the leadership teams can see value and impact of internal communication there has to be alignment of purpose.

7 There are some foundations for impactful communication; focusing on the audience, setting clear goals, getting the tone right, keeping it simple, structure to messaging, adapting to the medium.

8 The channel mix for the organization needs to consider print, online and face to face, and it needs to be two-way. The range of channels on offer can feel overwhelming but use the matrix to map out what exists now, where the gaps are and how to change it to meet the needs of the organization.

9 Culture and how things get done inside the organization are intrinsically linked to communication – communication is how we do it, but the relationship is the output. The relationships and how we work together are culture.

10 A global crisis will impact culture, much as a change in leadership or organization-wide changes in technology do – they will all have an impact on how things get done and how people work together.

11 Employee engagement, internal communication and employee experience are all different – we need to stop using the terms interchangeably, but we do need to recognize how they fit together.

Working closely with HR and IT will help ensure that the communication is having impact across the organization.

12 The model to create an internal communication strategy has five phases: insight, business intelligence, principles, communication and measurement. You must start with data to inform the strategy and plan. The model can be used as a step-by-step guide or you can combine the insight and business intelligence phases.

13 Data tells us that internal communication sits in the PR and corporate communication function.

14 Communication can be the cause of chaos. Having channels, tools and a plan in place to ensure communication is open and transparent will help you move out of chaos and into calm.

Quick tips

- Make sure you are clear what the organization's strategy is to ensure that the communication strategy can be measured in line with it.

- Understand the culture you want to achieve to enable you to use the right channels to support it.

- Ensure the leadership team are aligned to a common strategy and message.

- Have a good foundation of channels – the way you communicate with employees is so important and they need to be two-way.

- Invest in line managers' skills around communication – people work for people so the relationship here is key for engagement.

- Take the time to listen to employees and all internal stakeholders so you know what is really happening.

- Use a channel matrix to map out the way you communicate – it helps you to have a clear framework for the organization and avoids ambiguity.

References and further reading

CIMA (nd) CIMA – About us, www.cimaglobal.com/About-us/ (archived at https://perma.cc/Y2RL-LESP)

CIPD (2009) Our history, www.cipd.co.uk/about/who-we-are/history (archived at https://perma.cc/94FN-TAB3)

CIPR (nd) About PR, www.cipr.co.uk/CIPR/About_Us/About_PR (archived at https://perma.cc/5MBM-L493)

CIPR (2017) Making it count: The strategic value and effectiveness of internal communication, https://newsroom.cipr.co.uk/leaders-now-value-internal-comms---cipr-inside-report/ (archived at https://perma.cc/WWK3-49R3)

Dewhurst, S and Fitzpatrick, L (2019) *Successful Employee Communications: A practitioner's guide to tools, models and best practice for internal communication*, Kogan Page, London

Engage for Success (nd) What is Employee Engagement, https://engageforsuccess.org/what-is-employee-engagement (archived at https://perma.cc/PTJ3-Q4Q9)

Fitzpatrick, L and Valskov, K (2014) *Internal Communications: A manual for practitioners*, Kogan Page, London

Gatehouse (2020) State of The Sector, https://sots-dot-gallagher-indigo-storm-uk-apps.appspot.com/ (archived at https://perma.cc/RX3R-PQKF)

IoIC (nda) 2000s – IoIC History, https://ioictimeline.org.uk/2000s/ (archived at https://perma.cc/TPF6-GUHR)

IoIC (ndb) Why is internal communication important?, www.ioic.org.uk/about-ioic/why-is-ic-important (archived at https://perma.cc/TW2L-UKT4)

Lynn, N (2019) *Employee Experience (EX) Leadership: Build trust through employee experience and engagement*, independently published

Macleod, D and Clarke, N (2009) 'Engaging for Success: Enhancing performance through employee engagement', Department of Business, Information and Skills, https://engageforsuccess.org/wp-content/uploads/2015/08/file52215.pdf (archived at https://perma.cc/65JW-ZHC4)

Maylett, T and Wride, M (2017) *The Employee Experience: How to attract talent, retain top performers, and drive results*, Wiley, Hoboken, NJ

Moore, K (2011) Edgar Schein on Corporate Culture, YouTube, www.youtube.com/watch?v=6ZB3jJlGWuk (archived at https://perma.cc/2PZB-XZE5)

Morgan, J (2016) The Employee Experience Equation, Jacob Morgan, 25 February, https://thefutureorganization.com/the-employee-experience-equation/ (archived at https://perma.cc/YLJ3-BFD2)

Ruck, K and PR Academy (2012) *Exploring Internal Communication: Towards informed employee voice*, Pearson/Custom, Harlow

Wikipedia (2019a) Public Relations and Communications Association, Wikipedia, en.wikipedia.org/wiki/Public_Relations_and_Communications_Association (archived at https://perma.cc/45GX-8DSN)

Wikipedia (2019b) Chartered Institute of Public Relations, Wikipedia, en.wikipedia.org/wiki/Chartered_Institute_of_Public_Relations (archived at https://perma.cc/QP52-JC8Y)

Without communication there is chaos

02

In the first chapter we discussed the role of internal communication inside organizations, looking at frameworks, the link to culture and the relationship between communication and engagement.

In this chapter we will explore what chaos is inside organizations and why it needs to be explored as a fundamental aspect of modern work. A phrase we often hear is that change is the only constant. I'd argue that really, this is chaos. We have tried to package it in change and create roles and processes around change to help us manage systems and people but it doesn't always work.

When I write about chaos in organizations people often jump to a mental image of people running around, a major crisis under way and everyone in a state of panic. This rarely the case.

Chaos is all around us, all of the time. To take the Cambridge Dictionary definition, it is 'a total state of confusion with no order'.

Chaos theory in mathematics suggests that the apparent randomness of chaos is false. There are underlying patterns that show connections, patterns and loops. If we look at this idea alongside the dictionary definition, we can see how it can be applied to organizations.

Chaos is a state of utter confusion but there are patterns within that confusion that, if you explore and delve into, you can calm. Even where there is complexity, you can find the ability to bring control.

In organizations, chaos is everywhere because organizations are complex. They are complex because they involve people and in many cases they operate in multiple locations around the world as well. We bring order to this complexity with organizational charts and standard operating procedures, etc but elements of chaos will always exist.

What is chaos?

What does chaos look like? You might think that chaos doesn't apply to you. But chaos can take many forms.

This is a conversation I had in a previous role where I was trying to understand how things happened in order to move things forward. The conversation shows not only a chaotic way of working but also hinted at an underlying issue that compounded the chaos internally:

Boss: 'We work at pace here so bear in mind that things move quickly.'

Me: 'That's no problem, I'm used to pace so I have no issue here.'

Me: 'What's the process to get the presentation together for the management meeting?'

Boss: 'We have individual meetings 1:1, then smaller groups and then two pre-meetings followed by a post-management meeting.'

This isn't pace. This is inefficient process born out of fear of being challenged. This isn't an agile organization, it's one bogged down in the need to prepare for every possible eventuality. Even worse, in this case there was a clear message that the organization was transparent and open, but the processes and ways of working signalled something very different.

When it comes to organizations, this is chaos. It might not be people running around and things tumbling down – but it is chaos. There is confusion and disorder – the very definition of chaos. The meanings of many words in use today have shifted or been exaggerated. Chaos is one of them. When I'm describing chaos in organizations today, these are some examples of what I mean:

Complete focus on financial aspects of business:

– There is little mention of people, strategy or how it all links together.

Inability to get work done:

- Individuals and teams are unable to make decisions to move things forwards and continue to work on things in ways that aren't aligned to organizational goals.

Lots of meetings without things moving forward:

- Time spent together to discuss things with the wrong people in the room, a lack of good meeting management and therefore inefficient use of time.

People off on stress/sick leave:

- This leaves work for the wider team to pick up, adding more stress and leave. This becomes cyclical as the leaders fail to tackle the issue.

Recovering from a global crisis:

- Rebalancing an organization after significant disruption to the normal ways of working.

High turnover of employees:

- A lack of leaving interviews and understanding around what is causing the issues leads to sweeping them under the carpet. It leads to a view that people are always replaceable.

Merger/acquisition in progress:

- Lots of change for everyone, causing high levels of ambiguity and often a lack of information. Fast pace and time-consuming for leadership.

Rewarding senior leaders too much:

- Lack of fairness throughout the organization with a focus on senior leaders – this could lead to organizational failure and administration.

Team friction:

- Different teams are not getting on, causing issues with winning business, efficiency, working together and a lack of respect.

Loss of purpose:

- Lack of clarity around why the organization exists and therefore how employees connect what they do to something bigger.

Lack of connection to the front-line employees who interface with customers:

- Lack of two-way dialogue with those on the front line leaves them confused about what is happening, feeling like 'just a number' and not cared about.

Large investment in communication campaigns that address these things but don't make any difference:

- Doing all the right things but not measuring them against real objectives, and not recognizing the lack of change.

Lack of commercial understanding from senior leaders:

- Focusing on management rather than leadership without understanding consequences of actions or decisions.

Toxic chaos

I know there are many people who will say that you need chaos to enable change. Or that you need it for innovation and creativity. And to some degree you do. You need to be able to have freedom to think and explore and do things differently to ignite changes inside organizations but this doesn't have to mean a chaotic system and an out of control organization.

Glassdoor is a website where employees can leave reviews for the organizations they work for. Organizations place varying degrees of weight or focus on what is written, but it can be a good place to hear honest feedback about an organization.

In August 2020, an employee wrote about toxic chaos in their organization and cited the following 'cons' to working there:

- no effective management structure;
- no induction;

- all work allocated nationally by algorithm;
- no support for new staff;
- extremely high turnover of staff;
- sweatshop office conditions;
- crumbling and damp building;
- ancient IT hardware and software;
- atmosphere of fear, which prevents cooperation;
- IT support provided by external company based outside the UK;
- staff are 'resources' not individuals.

So when we look at chaos in a toxic sense we can see that this has a negative impact on the employee experience. There doesn't need to be chaos that is detrimental to well-being, efficiency or organizational success, and I believe there is a need for this distinction.

In a similar way to making a distinction between things like blame and accountability or shame and guilt, there are things that are similar but create very different outcomes and emotions in people.

If an organization is chaotic and there is high turnover or no effective management structure, then the chaos is toxic. If there is chaos in the sense that there is a fast pace and people come up with ideas to innovate and drive change, and it feels like there is always something moving around – this isn't toxic. There is control and balance, and that is what we need to strive for.

As people change and move around into different roles or places the relationships inside also change. In addition, business focus might shift and as a result the processes around these things will change too. If we don't talk about the balance and control needed as things start to become toxic, we can lose people for good.

You can sometimes see the toxicity play out in behaviours, especially in meetings. This can be in the form of microaggressions or silent vetoes (people agree in the room but disagree outside the room, when with their peers). This has a huge link to the culture of the organization and it's why we can link chaos and communication together so strongly.

We can see toxic chaos in large organizations in articles in the press. In the following case studies you can see that things can go unchecked and the inevitable happens. The roles of purpose and chaos can be seen, as when the purpose starts to falter and the focus shifts, chaos is created.

There are lots of ways things could have ended differently for the brands in the case studies but what is important is that we recognize there are two types of chaos – the balanced chaos that engenders creativity and innovation, and the negative, toxic chaos that leaves employees feeling anxious, unappreciated and unproductive.

This cannot continue. There is a lot that needs to change in organizations and it has to start with communication and relationships.

When you're only 'making tomorrow a better place' for the directors

Leadership teams sometimes exhibit an astonishing lack of rationale in relation to remuneration strategy. The demise of construction and facilities giant Carillion is a classic example of the chaos resulting from blindly rewarding senior leaders.

Following its compulsory liquidation in January 2018, the UK's Parliamentary Business Committee reported on Carillion's collapse. They described a 'relentless dash for cash' and leaders who exhibited a 'reckless short-termism', focusing on pay deals and bonuses, rather than commercial sustainability and delivering contracts.

Richard Howson was CEO from 2012 until July 2017 when he left following a shock profit warning. He earned £1.5 million in 2016, with the addition of a £122,612 cash bonus and £231,000 in pension contributions. On resignation, the company agreed to continue paying him a £660,000 annual salary and £28,000 in benefits until October 2018. Keith Cochrane, who replaced Howson as interim CEO, was due to receive his £750,000 annual salary until July 2018. A similar deal was in place for former finance director Zafar Khan, who stepped down in September 2017.

Downfalls like Carillion's don't just happen overnight and the joint enquiry found evidence that failures had taken place over many years. KPMG audited Carillion for 19 years, earning £29 million in the process. To say effective governance was lacking is an understatement.

In the years preceding its collapse the company went from crisis to crisis, but never took stock. In 2017 there were three profit warnings in five months. When four large contracts ran into trouble, the company continued to be awarded vital government contracts for hospitals, schools and transport infrastructure. It was working on 420 public sector projects when it went bust.

Carillion built up £7 billion in liabilities but continued to pay investors their dividends and limited the criteria under which executive bonuses could be repaid. Roger Barker, Head of Corporate Governance at the Institute of Directors said: 'The relaxation of clawback conditions for executive bonuses in 2016 appears in retrospect to be highly inappropriate' (Davies, 2018).

This truly was rewards for failure.

With only £29 million in the bank, Carillion took on too much, too cheaply. The Government ignored the signs and, as the Parliamentary report stated, Carillion 'danced to the Government's tune, focusing on delivering on price, not service; volume not value.'

Clearly the system was as defective as the business leaders and this raises questions about private companies performing public services, where contracts have tight margins. Interim CEO Keith Cochrane admitted that: 'In too many cases, we were building a Rolls-Royce but only getting paid to build a Mini.'

Thankfully, the directors had their payments halted by the liquidator; little comfort to the 43,000 global employees and subcontractors who were owed up to £1 billion in retentions.

Executive reward does have its power, but also has its downsides. Where long-term strategic planning towards sustainable growth was needed, Carillion instead disintegrated under the self-serving tendencies of executives and increasing pressure from investors to deliver. At no point did the board attempt to reduce debt or consolidate the business. The payouts allowed recipients to gain rewards while the company was in financial difficulty. The chaos was created by individuals and, I would suspect, leadership that was grounded in a way of leading linked to factory and production workers rather than what's needed for the modern organization today.

A focus on costs is often a driver for a change in organizational strategy. This can, in turn, create chaos as the norm is disrupted and employees are confused. We will explore the role of employee engagement and strategic narrative later in the book but it is here where things can start to diminish.

How cost-cutting on croissants caused burnt fingers for iconic patisserie

Patisserie Valerie is renowned for its fresh croissants, millefeuille and tarte tatin; all made with a sinful – but essential – amount of butter. The classic French patisserie, which opened its first store in London's Soho in 1926, prided itself on its handmade sweet treats. It developed a reputation as a unique meeting place for the arts scene.

When the original site was bombed in 1941, the resilient founder quickly reopened in Old Compton Street and continued to expand significantly. Before falling dramatically into administration in October 2018, Patisserie Valerie appeared to be riding high, with a value of £450 million, nearly 200 stores and a team of 3,000.

In the background, it was making a loss on its cakes.

When a business hits serious financial difficulty, rapid cost-cutting is often critical to its survival. While this is a sensible strategy, it must be done without losing the core purpose of the business; in this case selling delicious, premium pastries. Most famously, Patisserie Valerie managers were found to have introduced cost-cutting so harsh they had replaced butter with margarine in puff pastry.

Just a few months later, its accounts were found to have a £94 million 'black hole' following 'potentially fraudulent accounting irregularities'. Luke Johnson, former Executive Chairman and largest shareholder when it collapsed, said he had no knowledge of alleged fraud and that accounts had appeared healthy. Five people were arrested following the scandal and the case was subject to a Serious Fraud Office investigation. Around 900 café staff lost their jobs.

In early 2019, Patisserie Valerie was rescued by Causeway Capital Partners, who bought the company out of administration. It paid a meagre £5 million for 100 cafés, a quarter of which it subsequently closed. Partner Matt Scaife said the business had been 'seriously mismanaged'. They found broken ovens, unpaid suppliers and a leaky roof at a key site.

Patisserie Valerie's current Managing Director, Paolo Peretti, is planning to get the company back on track, with £1 million investment in revamping cafés and new sites planned. The butter is back, along with a new menu. Mr Peretti admits the 'lurid headlines about fraud and missing millions are not going to help.'

This is an unfortunate example of what can happen when lack of clarity about why an organization exists in the first place causes it to lose its core purpose. It's clear there were several factors at play but cutting corners on ingredients in a premium patisserie will no doubt have damaged the authenticity of the brand.

Chaos is not people running around in mild or crazy panic. It's about a lack of alignment, a lack of focus, lack of awareness and an overall lack of understanding. To bring a sense of calm is to bring simplicity to something that is no doubt complex. The case studies show how chaos can appear to come out of nowhere, how it can slowly build and how it can easily take control.

There are so many case studies that show how organizations can fall victim to 'toxic chaos'. The staff emails that are leaked to the press. The brand ratings based on their response to employee treatment during the Covid-19 pandemic. The ethical behaviour of leaders around the world. The risk to reputation, the risk for shareholders and the risk to the bottom line are gradually making their way to the top of the list. Investing in influential and effective internal communication will be the difference between success and failure in the long term. For some this might be seen as the softer side of business but without it, things won't get into an order that will enable you to manage the chaos.

Managing chaos

Chaos without management is toxic and will cause many of the symptoms we have already listed in this chapter.

Chaos and constant change are the same thing. We do live in a world where things are often changing but we are also able to find ways to control that to enable people to be productive and organizations to be efficient. There is a normal turbulence to organizations.

This comes from the involvement of people, and in organizations today, the need to adapt management styles and leadership to the world of work in 2020 and beyond needs a closer look.

Later in this book we will explore the role of leadership and chaos. We will look at the different types of leadership and how people can, and need to, adapt to support organizations today.

Here we can explore the theory of management philosophies alongside chaos: managing by instruction, managing by objectives and managing by values:

- Managing by instruction (MBI) links back to the manufacturing and assembly-line work and the management of teams and individuals on a more instruction/task basis. This was around the turn of the 20th century.

- Management by objectives (MBO) was introduced in the 1960s when long-term goals for organizations was a trend. This is linked to goal-setting, motivating individuals behind an objective. A trend that continues today.

- Management by values (MBV) builds on MBO by exploring the common goal and the values of an organization. It links to cultures and leaders who look at a more strategic change for the organization – it's about everyone in the organization having a shared purpose and agreed value set.

In Table 2.1 you can see how the different management philosophies are demonstrated against different situations.

Type of leadership is a great one to bring the three differences to life – you can see the different styles under each management philosophy and the shift from traditional to transformational. In addition, the philosophy of control shows how the role of management links to chaos. From top-down to encouragement, it's starting to get easier to see how things needs to shift inside organizations to manage chaos.

As we look at managing chaos you can draw on the different management styles to see how to move to a place of control. Chaos will always exist to some degree but shifting the control to encouragement of individual development, the vision to long-term, and the

Table 2.1   Comparison between MBI, MBO and MBV from Dolan, Garcia, and Auerbach (2003)

	MBI	MBO	MBV
Preferable situation for application	Routine or emergencies	Moderate complexity Relatively 'standardized' production	Need for creativity in the solution of complex problems
Average level of professionalism of members of the organization	Basic level of instruction (management of operatives)	Moderate average professionalism (management of employees)	High level of average professionalism (management of professionals)
Type of leadership	Traditional	Allocator of resources	Transformational (value shaper)
Image of customer	User–buyer	User–customer	Customer with judgement and freedom of choice
Type of product market	Monopolist Standardized	Segmented	Highly diversified and dynamic
Type of organizational structure	Pyramidal with many levels	Pyramidal with few levels	Networks, functional alliances, project team structures
Need for tolerance of ambiguity	Low	Medium	High
Need for autonomy and responsibility	Low	Medium	High
Stability of environment	Stable	Moderately changeable	Very dynamic and changeable
Social organization	Capitalist-industrial	Capitalist post-industrial	Post-capitalist
Philosophy of control	'Top-down' control and supervision	Control and stimulus of professional performance	Encouragement of self-control by each individual

Table 2.1 *continued*

	MBI	MBO	MBV
Purpose of the organization	Maintenance of production	Optimization of results	Continuous improvement of processes
Reach of strategic vision	Short term	Medium term	Long term
Basic cultural values	Quantitative production Loyalty Conformity Discipline	Rationalization Motivation Efficiency Measurement of results	Developing participation Continuous learning Creativity Mutual trust Commitment Enjoy work

cultural values to more creativity and agility, there is a clear way to change, to adapt, to manage.

The link between values and chaos is an interesting one. In organizations, this is particularly relevant because people are such a fundamental part of what makes an organization (more on this in Chapter 4). As the world of work changes and adapts to meet the needs of society and the growth of technology, the values of people and the human aspect to work can be diminished. This leads to chaos.

Chaos and values

There has been extensive work on the role values play in individuals. We have looked at the role of management, but we also need to look at the values inside organizations.

There is a lot of research around values and for many internal communicators there will be a set of values for the organization that are used to drive behaviours and the culture. As we look further into the research around chaos inside organizations, there are several categories values can be placed in.

When it comes to chaos, this is important because it is the values that create balance. We look to harmonize personal values with organizational values. Organizations will always have a purpose or a final, core value. How the organization behaves, or the behaviours of those in the organization will be paramount to the overall achievement of that purpose. These can be categorized as 'ethical' or 'competence' (Rokeach, 1973):

Ethical = conduct	Conduct = social values like honesty/integrity
Competence = individual characteristics	Individual characteristics = creativity/flexibility

These are important to note when it comes to chaos and people. There is a direct link here between the people who are recruited and the purpose of the organization. We so often recruit individuals based on skills and task but less so on social values (which link to conduct and ethics). It could be argued that these social values are more important than the task (in some roles) given the need for relationships to thrive in order for things to be efficient. This is not to say we should recruit people that are the same. The need for diversity in organizations is also proven to be a key part of success. But exploring the values of individuals in the recruitment process would help ensure everyone is behind the purpose.

Control and development

The competency values can be broken down further into control and development, and this is where the balance of the organization sits. This is the point where chaos or calm happens. Striking this balance is what most organizations will strive to do. Through a combination of process and management styles this balance is what keeps things turning:

Control = efficiency, responsibility, etc
Development = trust, freedom, etc

When you manage with a value-based system (MBV), the balance is easier to create. You're managing your team by putting the people first, not the task. In many organizations this balance is hard to find. The balance between efficiency and trust is hard and when individuals are working more flexibly, and remotely from an office, it is even harder. As we explore the different leadership styles and how they impact organizations we will see a link to this shift. A need to adapt how we lead and manage to mitigate chaos and bring balance to the organization.

While processes are needed to bring a sense of order and control, if there is no freedom, trust or development, the order won't be sustainable.

This can be seen in organizations where systems and controls are in place, but they aren't working. This is an example of a conversation I had with a client as we worked through the reasons why things weren't happening:

Me: 'We are going to need a different system to manage the business development through to pitch.'

Client: 'We have a process, people just don't follow it.'

Me: 'How long have you had the process for?'

Client: 'Years – they just don't follow it and if they did it would be much easier to get things done.'

Me: 'The process needs to change.'

This was promptly followed by the posters that outlined the process being removed from the walls.

You cannot keep beating the same drum that a process exists, and people need to follow it – that is management by instruction. People won't follow that, and they need to be part of the solution – they need to be trusted.

This is linked to motivation for employees, their engagement, how they feel at work, as well as the investment in systems and technology. The balance of control and development are key to the management of chaos.

Chaos will always exist inside organizations because they are complex. Finding a way to bring the balance between these value sets will enable the organization to thrive. This is easier said than done. And that's because organizations are people, and people are complex.

Chaos and communication

In the previous chapter we delved into internal communication and how it works inside organizations, but here we can start to see the thread between the two. As we go further into the book to look at people in more detail, the role of purpose and values – it will all come together to the solution of communication.

Chaos is confusion. Communication can combat confusion. It doesn't matter how complicated something might appear, a conversation, listening, communicating about it will help. When we are confused, we want to ask questions and we want to be heard. In organizations the role of the internal communicator is to facilitate that, ensuring people are engaged.

If we explore some of the elements discussed earlier in this chapter and toxic chaos, we can see how communication can be the antidote (see Table 2.2).

This is just a snapshot of the what the rest of this book will explore. It shows you how there are links to communication from almost every aspect of chaos that exists in the organization.

In this table there are references to accountability, responsibility, culture, motivation – all things that are linked to communication, and some that are much easier to write than do. For internal communication to be influential and effective we must follow the advice in Chapter 1. With insight and planning, we can put in foundations that give everyone the chance to communicate effectively.

The antidote will bring calm to the organization. This doesn't mean a slowness, which is sometimes the nervousness around the word – it brings things under control and it brings a sense of order to the chaos. Investing in communication as the antidote is an easy investment to make. We all communicate all the time so honing those skills to ensure relationships are working well and the organization is running efficiently should be an easy decision for investment.

Table 2.2   How can communication be the antidote to chaos

Chaos	Communication antidotes
Complete focus on financial aspects of business	Find the story that can be told linked to the purpose and the people
Inability to get work done	Talk about where the accountability is and the decision making – be clear on everybody's roles and responsibilities
Lots of meetings without things moving forward	Discuss the best way to make decisions, who is needed and when the best time to have the conversation is
People off on stress/sick leave	Listen to the people who are off and find out what is really going on
High turnover of employees	Conduct leaving interviews and examine trends
Merger/acquisition in progress	Define the culture of the new organization and communicate in a way that aligns to it – be open
Team friction	Discuss with each team member what is happening for them, and look at motivations for each person and how to get them working better together

The benefits of focusing on influential communication to bring calm will include:

- better productivity;
- increased profitability;
- growth of your team or organization;
- employee satisfaction;
- business longevity;
- agility.

Chaos and mindset

To be able to accept chaos inside an organization takes a certain mindset. Some will be blind to it; others will see and ignore it. The mindset to accept it, learn and adapt is not in every leader. To grow (and you could argue just to survive), there is a need to recognize and take action.

Work by Smith and Saint-Onge (1996) suggests that an organization needs to be evolutionary in approach, adopting a mindset that is comfortable with change and also the ability to influence habits, thinking and learning.

An evolutionary organization takes a systemic approach and as we have explored chaos in this chapter it is easy to see why this could be the solution. To bring the balance needed to control chaos there has to be a mindset that can work through things and see how balance can be created. As a leadership team this is imperative as a combined skill.

We can often forget about the need to be aware and able when it comes to change – it's being able that is so important. As we continue through the chapters in this book, we will explore the importance of understanding people and organizations in more detail. The understanding of people is not only relevant for the internal communicator, but it is also important for ourselves. We have to understand our own mindsets and our own blockers to moving forward.

When chaos hits, do we bury our heads, procrastinate and do anything to avoid it? Or do we recognize it and openly discuss the symptoms and possible reasons for its development? It is the mindset that avoids it that lands us in toxic chaos territory. This mindset is the main challenge organizations have. Part of this is linked to our inability to be vulnerable, which we will explore in more detail in Chapter 3.

The mindset has to focus on business outcomes and what needs to change in order to bring a sense of calm. It isn't always easy and as an internal communicator there is a need to have a greater understanding in this area. The role of the function is to advise and enable others, so there must be skills to help others overcome the fear of stepping forward. Skills to help people see what is going on and the skills to support them as they step into a place of accountability and ownership.

Key points in this chapter

1 Chaos is a state of utter confusion but there are patterns within that confusion which, if you explore and delve into, you can calm. Even where there is complexity, you can find the ability to bring control.

2 Chaos and constant change are the same thing. We do live in a world where things are often changing but we are also able to find ways to control that, to enable people to be productive and organizations to be efficient. We don't need to see change as a constant; it should have a start and an end.

3 Chaos can be seen in organizations where people are off on stress/sick leave, teams aren't working well together, leadership are not commercially minded. It's not about people running around and being in a state of panic.

4 Some chaos can aid creativity and innovation, but toxic chaos will lead to a challenging work environment and a toxic culture.

5 Aim to adopt the management philosophy of management by values (MBV). It links to cultures and leaders who look at a more strategic change for the organization and should also align to common goals for the organization.

6 Adjusting your management approach to be value-led ensures you can focus everyone on the same direction and motivate them in line with both personal and organizational values.

7 Processes designed with control only won't work. People won't follow something they haven't been trusted to create – they need to be part of the solution.

8 Communicating openly will be the best antidote to chaos because it provides space for control and trust to work together in balance.

9 Resolving chaos has to be led from the top and as a team to ensure there is a clear and consistent approach to shifting to a more values-led culture.

10 We have to see the organization as evolutionary with a desire to change. Mindset is key for the leadership of the organization – they have to be willing to recognize and change.

11 The skills of the communicator have to support the leadership team, with better understanding of chaos and impact and how to mitigate it.

Quick tips

- Identify the types of chaos you have in your organization from the examples listed in this chapter.
- Take the time to explore how long they have been there and use your experience to consider why they exist.
- Think about balance and freedom and what's needed to shift to management by values over management by instruction or objective.
- If you have data on employee engagement, look at it through the lens of chaos.

References and further reading

Blackhurst, C (2018) Carillion collapse: A flawed system is to blame more than management excess, *Independent*, 22 January, www.independent. co.uk/news/business/comment/carillion-collapse-public-sector-partnerships-pfi-managers-pay-income-a8168086.html (archived at https://perma.cc/SLW5-X6MW)

Brignall, M (2019) Cash-starved Patisserie Valerie 'stopped using butter in puff pastry', *Guardian*, 16 June, www.theguardian.com/business/2019/jun/16/cash-starved-patisserie-valerie-stopped-using-butter-in-puff-pastry (archived at https://perma.cc/56YR-9R3M)

Building (2019) Carillion one year on: How the contractor's collapse unfolded, www.building.co.uk/focus/carillion-one-year-on-how-the-contractors-collapse-unfolded/5097348.article (archived at https://perma.cc/K8VS-4T9W)

Butler, S. (2019) Putting butter back in the pastry: Patisserie Valerie's road to recovery, *Guardian*, 12 December, www.theguardian.com/business/2019/dec/12/patisserie-valerie-cafe-cake-shop-chain-collapse-road-to-recovery-paolo-peretti (archived at https://perma.cc/VUE8-HWM9)

Cambridge Dictionary (nd) Chaos (definition), dictionary.cambridge.org/dictionary/english/chaos (archived at https://perma.cc/B4U2-8G5G)

Curry, R (2018) Carillion directors have payments pulled as Government agrees wage deal for private sector workers, *Telegraph*, 17 January, www.telegraph.co.uk/business/2018/01/17/government-agrees-wage-deal-90pc-carillions-private-clients/ (archived at https://perma.cc/S7VN-6MJJ)

Davies, R (2018) Carillion bosses prioritised pay over company affairs, MPs hear, *Guardian*, 7 March, www.theguardian.com/business/2018/mar/07/carillion-bosses-prioritised-pay-over-company-affairs-mps-hear (archived at https://perma.cc/M2G3-7ZWT)

Dolan, S L, Garcia, S and Auerbach, A (2003) Understanding and managing chaos in organisations, *International Journal of Management*, 20 (1), www.researchgate.net/profile/Simon_Dolan/publication/265748021_Understanding_and_managing_chaos_in_organisations/links/54d903c10cf2970e4e7a8b06/Understanding-and-managing-chaos-in-organisations.pdf (archived at https://perma.cc/E26P-98XY)

Glassdoor (nd) BPP Holdings – Toxic chaos, www.glassdoor.co.uk/Reviews/Employee-Review-BPP-Holdings-RVW35052758.htm (archived at https://perma.cc/8PY3-JQ6H)

Goodley, S (2018) Carillion's 'highly inappropriate' pay packets criticized, *Guardian*, 15 January, www.theguardian.com/business/2018/jan/15/carillion-highly-inappropriate-pay-packets-criticised (archived at https://perma.cc/3Q7Q-VUV9)

Morris, B (2019) Patisserie Valerie: unravelling the history of the café chain, BBC News, 6 February, www.bbc.co.uk/news/business-47094831 (archived at https://perma.cc/NU7M-UY7D)

Patisserie Valerie (nd) Our story, www.patisserie-valerie.co.uk/pages/about-us (archived at https://perma.cc/83YK-CKQ3)

Prezi (2014) The evolutionary organization: Avoiding a Titanic fate, 15 April, prezi.com/w2aiu67ejagp/the-evolutionary-organization-avoiding-a-titanic-fate/ (archived at https://perma.cc/WV2C-SUCN)

Rokeach, M (1973) *The Nature of Human Values*, Free Press, New York

Smith, P A C and Saint-Onge, H (1996) The evolutionary organization: Avoiding a *Titanic* fate, *The Learning Organization*, 3 (4), pp 4–21

Titcomb, J (2018) £7bn in Carillion liabilities revealed, *Telegraph*, 14 April, www.telegraph.co.uk/business/2018/04/14/7bn-carillion-debts-revealed/ (archived at https://perma.cc/MWK2-9MA5)

The Construction Index (2018) Carillion report: Conclusions and recommendations, 16 May, www.theconstructionindex.co.uk/news/view/carillion-report-conclusions-and-recommendations (archived at https://perma.cc/94UX-TTBX)

Thomas, D (2018) Where did it go wrong for Carillion? BBC News, 15 January, www.bbc.co.uk/news/business-42666275 (archived at https://perma.cc/4KVK-QKDN)

UK Parliament (2018) Carillion – Business, Energy and Industrial Strategy and Work and Pensions Committees – House of Commons, publications.parliament.uk/pa/cm201719/cmselect/cmworpen/769/76908.htm (archived at https://perma.cc/46GY-SQ7X)

UK Parliament (nd) Carillion joint inquiry, publications.parliament.uk/pa/cm201719/cmselect/cmworpen/769/769.pdf (archived at https://perma.cc/VK2X-VABR)

Wikipedia (nd) Patisserie Valerie, en.wikipedia.org/wiki/Patisserie_Valerie (archived at https://perma.cc/VK9A-PZ5E)

Wikipedia (2019) Chaos theory, en.wikipedia.org/wiki/Chaos_Theory (archived at https://perma.cc/W5SY-DZGR)

Wood, Z (2019) Patisserie Valerie accounts black hole now £94m, says KPMG, *Guardian*, 15 March, www.theguardian.com/business/2019/mar/15/patisserie-valerie-accounts-black-hole-94m-say-kpmg (archived at https://perma.cc/WH7G-VA96)

Understanding organizations and leadership 03

An organization is not a real thing. They are myths. The tangible, literal aspects of an organization are the assets (buildings, cars, etc) and the people. But the 'organization' is something we have created.

There is a lot of theory linked to organizations and it tends to work in parallel with management theory – cementing the view that the organization is not a real thing and that it is actually about the people inside it.

Henry Mintzberg, Canadian academic and scholar, suggested a model that shows the configuration of an organization. He suggested there are six basic components to an organization:

1 Strategic apex (top management)

2 Middle line (middle management)

3 Operating core (operations, operational processes)

4 Technostructure (systems, processes)

5 Support staff (support, usually based in an office)

6 Ideology (beliefs, values, culture)

These component parts are very accurate for most organizations today. Whether there are seven of you or thousands of you, the organizational structure will usually mimic something like this.

When it comes to internal communication, the size of the organization is irrelevant. People often say 'when there are only a few of you it's much easier to communicate'. This isn't true. Whether working with organizations that consist of 90,000 people or 10 people, some of the challenges are the same. This is often down to the relationships in the teams or across the organization, the lack of processes that have been put in place or the ideology/purpose being unclear.

In this chapter we will look at the aspects of organizations today that need to be explored to ensure you can have influential internal communication. This includes the role of community inside organizations, globalization, the different generations in the workplace and the rate of change. All of these organizational elements need to be explored for internal communication to succeed.

In Chapter 1 we talked about the model for internal communication strategy and planning. The second part of that model related to business intelligence, which is what this chapter is going to look at. To understand the organization, there are some questions that should always be asked when looking at the communication flow:

- Is it a global organization with employees working in different time zones and physical locations?
- Do people work shifts?
- Is it a Monday to Friday 9 am to 5 pm organization?
- Are people digitally connected or are they working with customers face to face?
- Is it growing through mergers and acquisitions?
- Is there a strong sense of brand and purpose across the organization?
- Is everyone in one office? Is that office open plan?

These are just a few to consider and with the impact of Covid-19 on organizations there will be more to ask as time goes on. Understanding how an organization came to exist, how it grows and how it needs to operate is so important when it comes to ensuring that strategies are in place for communication to be aligned to organizational goals.

Using the organizational chart will not help you understand communication. Continuing with the work of Mintzberg, he partnered with Ludo Van der Hayden to create 'organigraphs', or structure charts, designed to better reflect how organizations operate and to move us away from focusing on organizational charts as the visual representation of the business. These were developed over 20 years ago and yet today, we are still obsessed with the organizational charts that depict hierarchy and nothing else. The chart is just one piece of the organizational puzzle. It doesn't tell you who talks to who to get what done. It doesn't tell you where people are located and it doesn't tell you what they actually do. So we have to ask – how helpful are they really?

For the internal communicator, they are a good map of relationships. They show teams, line management and leadership, and while it is just one component part, it is one that we need to look at alongside the flow of communication and internal processes.

Leadership

Leadership and communication go hand in hand. As a leader, your role is to lead others and create a sense of followership, and to do this, your ability to influence others and effectively communicate is paramount.

There are more books than you can count about leadership, and they all have slightly different views on what good looks like.

Leaders come in all forms. There isn't one size for everyone; some have clear visions, some can clearly articulate how this plays out to the front line, others are eccentric and some want to lead through control while others bury their heads and hide away from talking to others. So much is linked to communication but importantly, so much has to be linked to being genuine.

There isn't just one book that is going to help but there is a need to understand the impact of your own leadership style on those who work for you. Whether you are a leader on paper, on the organizational chart or leading a project – the style with which you engage those around you will have an impact on success.

There are examples all around us, every day. From TV shows to films you can see the different styles of leaders and their impact on the workplace – just because something is fiction, it doesn't mean there isn't a real version.

Many of the styles link to leadership theory, and when we look at leadership today it's easy to see how many people leading organizations take advice from theories that existed when organizations were not the knowledge-based work they often are today.

Frederick Taylor's theory of scientific management is everywhere in organizations. His ideas are based on the need for consistency, hierarchy and efficiency. These founding principles are not wrong and the system he created to support organizations to make things more efficient and more productive cannot be faulted. But this was in a world of manufacturing. A world of hierarchy and a very different society to what we see today. Some of the principles remain sound but many are not suitable for the office environment and the knowledge workers who exist today.

To lead isn't to change

The challenge with many of the books about leadership is the focus on the need for the leader to create change to create impact.

Looking at the role of leadership in comparison to managing, it could be argued that we have created one of the biggest issues in business today. Leaders do not always need to transform or change a business. The defining trait for leaders should not be their ability to transform and yet everything we are teaching people today is exactly that.

As a leader you should inspire, challenge and demonstrate a vision that people can follow but this doesn't necessarily mean you need to change everything. We spent years under the belief that Taylorism was the solution (more people to make more boxes without allowing them any individual/original thought or two-way dialogue) and while we now know that isn't always right, creating a generation of leaders who believe that they need to change everything to be successful is equally wrong.

Change is an epidemic inside our organizations today. Talk to any team in any organization and they will tell you they are juggling several change programmes. We have change specialists and change teams and change management courses – the list goes on. Change is a perfectly normal part of life – both business and personal – and managing it does require skills, but it shouldn't require a team of people on a continual basis. If it does, that is just business as usual. It tells us the skills needed for the roles is different, or there are other skills that are a priority.

If you're taking a change-first approach to leadership then the need to understand people is paramount. Change for the sake of change will never create a long-term foundation for an organization. Many leaders enter the workplace with a desire to make a statement or to put their mark on things but without a reason to do that, it is just change without reason. Change needs to start with people. Understanding people, how they think, what drives them, etc, will be imperative to a change programme's success. Alongside people, make sure that you are exploring all elements of data and leadership as you explore your impact on the organization and your communication style that is working alongside this.

Servant leadership

The *New Amsterdam* series on Amazon Prime launched in 2019. It's about Dr Max Goodwin taking over a hospital in the United States. And anything like this will always get me interested because I'm keen to see how new leaders make a difference. I absolutely love the approach – it's incredibly simple, and it has been around since the 1950s when philosopher Robert Greenleaf introduced the concept of servant leadership.

Dr Goodwin opens the staff meeting with the question 'how can I help?' He clearly articulates that he wants to remove barriers that are in the way of success and he wants to hear what they are. While this takes a while to gain traction, the desire to listen, make changes, be on the side of employees who feel they are just a number will always demonstrate a level of empathy that can so often be lacking when it's head-down and numbers focused.

The key word here is empathy. The need to better understand emotions in the workplace and have the intelligence to understand people is why we have a whole chapter about understanding people.

Servant leadership is about being a leader who serves.

Accountability

We need to get uncomfortable before we get comfortable. Over the years our ability to be accountable has diminished. We are quick to blame others for our behaviour and we are quick to pass the buck when things go wrong. The ability to own decisions and consequences is paramount for leadership – and yet it is not available in abundance at any level.

Yuval Noah Harari, author of *Sapiens*, references how things have changed and where accountability may have gone wrong. Years ago, you might speak to an individual craftsperson to buy a cart because their trade is carpentry. You might buy this from them or trade with them for something you want. If the cart broke, you would go back to them and discuss what happened, how they could help fix it. The craftsperson was wholly accountable for the product and service. Today, we have created barriers. We have created 'organizations' so when things go wrong, the 'organization' is to blame. But what is the 'organization'? It's people, buildings, products – it is all those things that we can tangibly see wrapped up in something mythical that doesn't exist. This creation of an 'organization' has allowed us to put a barrier between ourselves and consequence – and we see it too often. We see it in the customer experience; the way customers are treated, the challenge it can be to reach a person to speak to when you want to ask a question, complain or simply get in touch.

The missing skills of managers

Managers often become managers because they are excellent at the task. It is rare for someone to become a manager if they aren't competent at completing the core task of the function and therein lies the challenge. The role of the manager is to manage the team. Spend time with them, guide them and help them. Communication is a fundamental skill needed and yet it is the skill that is rarely trained and invested in.

As a manager you have to connect on a human level. And while the relationship with people in your team will be different depending on what you do, making time for people and listening is incredibly important. We covered the importance of listening to others in Chapter 1 and this is where you can see the need for it more.

The missing skills of managers

Make time

I conduct a lot of interviews and 1:1s with team members – whether it is to prep for a workshop with a senior team or to help understand why things aren't getting done. During these sessions my focus is on that individual completely and I allow two hours for the conversation (on average). This is part of my role and as a manager it is part of yours. Make time for your team, really listen to them and help them overcome challenges (put your phone away, take notes, prep for the meeting). Recognize their achievements and work with them to help them achieve their own goals and aspirations.

If you don't know how, ask for help

I see many managers managing people because they are really good at the tasks involved in the job. They have had little training in how to manage and they have had even less exposure to the importance of communication in that relationship. I am a firm believer in continuous learning and in doing so, I have a network of people I can lean on and resources I know I can go to for help. This isn't a weakness, it is a necessity for me to be able to be help coach, mentor and lead in what I do.

Be accountable and make others accountable

Make sure that what you say and what you do are the same. A few years ago, the Edelman Trust Barometer highlighted such a gap in business. Being aware of this gap and its impact can really change relationships and cultures in the workplace. If you say you'll be at a meeting at 10, be at the meeting at 10. Consistent behaviour builds trust and enhances individual credibility.

Research from the Remotely Interested report (2019) into communicating with deskless workers showed that the line manager as a communicator is so important that it impacts the effectiveness of all other communication channels in the organization.

The data shows that the channel and content is actually irrelevant if the manager is not a good communicator – so if there is one thing that will help communication inside your organization, it's investment in line managers and their communication skills. Small tweaks can make a huge difference to efficiency and productivity in the workplace. As a leader, investing in your team's communication skills will be so important to success. Individual relationships in the workplace, between an employee and a line manager are fundamental to a good employee experience. This in turn means that the relationships need to be good and all relationships require strong communication to work well. We don't often consider this in the workplace but the data tells us that the line manager's skills in communication have such an impact that not providing budget and time to support this skill development will be detrimental to the organization both short and long term.

The importance of emotion

Simon Sinek has written and spoken extensively about leadership. His theories and books are often referenced as he identifies the things that will actually make a difference to people inside organizations.

In 2014 he spoke about leadership and the military, asking the question about whether certain roles attract certain types of leaders. He asks the question: where do leaders that have an emotional connection with their teams comes from?

Is it about the people? The individuals? No, it is the environment they work in.

Why risk everything to save someone else? Because that person would do the same for me – it's about trust and cooperation. But trust and cooperation are a feeling – I cannot tell you to trust me and know that you will. Like any feeling, the behaviour is what drives the shift and there are traits and things people can do to create a place of trust:

- Being genuine and authentic – and being consistent in your style and approach;
- Being trustworthy – if someone tells you something in confidence, it stays in confidence;
- Having integrity – say you will do something, and do it;
- Reliability;
- Empathy.

To keep that organization alive and safe from the 'dangers' outside, a leader that creates an environment of trust is a leader that will create a great organization. If an employee follows the rules because they fear for their job, it doesn't make for a great worker and it won't make for a successful company. All of this can be classed as psychological safety, a phrase that is gaining traction with organizations, following research into team effectiveness when there is no fear.

Sinek goes on to compare leaders to parents. 'We want the same for our children as we do for our employees: Opportunity, education, we discipline them when necessary all so they can grow up and achieve more than we could ourselves' (Sinek and Yates, 2017).

There is a big difference between being an authority and having authority over people, and being a leader and having people follow you. Just like there is a balance between power with and power over others. All of it links us back to trust and the way we can make people feel – and all of that comes back to how we communicate. The words we use, our body language and our tone all combined make up the complete communication. To be effective and influential, to create the safe place where people trust each other, support each other and work as a team we need to be able to communicate in a way that does exactly that.

Six leadership skills to master

1. Compassion

This feels like something leaders are often told they don't need but research shows that vulnerability and courage go hand in hand. And with that, comes compassion. We are all human and showing some of that in the workplace leads to more genuine relationships and more trust.

2. Look after yourself

One of the best book titles I have come across is *Your Oxygen Mask First* (Lawrence, 2017), because it is exactly that approach that is needed. You are the most important and you need to focus on your health and well-being to be able to lead others. Whether that's half an hour of yoga in the morning or five minutes – do what you can but make time for you, every day.

3. Respect

This works both ways. It works every way. Respect has to be given to everyone regardless of hierarchy. For some this comes naturally and for others this feels alien. Respect the time and expertise of others, you hired them for a reason.

4. Time and attention management – yours and others'

You can only listen to someone speak for 20 minutes before the brain wants to do something else. And the optimal time for you to focus is around 52 minutes with a 17-minute break. You need to focus your attention, not your time. The meetings are needed, the conversations are needed so focus your attention on what will make a difference, it's not about time.

5. Self-awareness

Knowing your limits is a huge strength in leadership. It's hard to show vulnerability and let someone know you need help, but find your trusted circle and use them to help you navigate and grow. No one expects you to do this alone so make sure you know when to ask for help.

6. Listening

Listening to those around you is a hugely important skill for leaders. Your response when someone is sharing or talking has more weight than that of a peer. Remember that how you show you're listening is equally important – are you making notes, eye contact, etc? How do they know you are listening and that you care?

Community

A community is often seen as a group of people who get together with shared values or a shared goal. When we think of a community, we might think of a community hall where there are local clubs for parents and babies, and dance classes for children, or coffee shops for people to gather in to chat.

We don't often think of community in terms of an organization.

The reason community is part of our society is because since the dawn of time, it has been at the core of the human race.

Yuval Noah Harari talks about our need for gossip, the myths of the organization and the optimal size for a community to thrive. Communities thrive when they all have a strong belief. In fact, this belief can be so strong that there is no need for laws or processes when the number of people in the community is fewer than 150.

Consider organizations today with 150 employees. And consider the organizational structure and hierarchy that they have put in place. It could be suggested that those things are in place because there is no one belief that binds them all as one community – no clear and believed purpose.

Robin Dunbar, a British anthropologist, calculated that 150 is the optimal size of social groupings for humans. The theory is based on brain size and average social group size. He suggests that anything larger than 150 requires laws, processes and other norms to create stability.

For an organization of this size, the only way to ensure there is a community inside it, with a solid belief and an ability to work together, is to look at the way the people communicate, and the processes that help it operate.

This isn't to say that when you have more than 150 people in a group you cannot have the belief and purpose – you absolutely can. But over 150 you do need structure and hierarchy.

The importance of purpose is one we will explore further throughout this book. Simon Sinek suggests leaders need to 'Start with Why'. His book of the same name covers the importance of articulating why you do what you do. In his TED Talk in 2009 about inspirational leadership, he shared his theory of the 'Golden Circle' where the outer ring is 'what', the middle ring is 'how' and the inner ring is 'why'. It is his theory that all successful individuals or organizations are successful because they lead with their why, then the how and the what follow.

Sinek will say he has simply codified this into this formula but the importance of why, social purpose and the growing need for people to feel part of something bigger than profit suggests it is grounded in a deep understanding of being human.

Being human means we want to be part of a group. We are social animals and social connection is incredibly important to us. As a group or a community, we are bonded by gossip. Gossip has a terrible reputation as rumour-mongering and negative news – to be a gossip is seen as a bad thing when in fact, it's an innate way for us to bond as a community or tribe. It is about us sharing thoughts and ideas and things that possibly don't even exist. The ability to communicate through ideas, myths or legends is unique to *Homo sapiens* – it's part of the reason we have survived for so long and it's why we have been able to take over the planet to become the top of the chain.

When it comes to organizations, understanding the reasons why gossip is innate is important but it's the size of the group or tribe that is imperative to understand when it comes to effective and influential communication.

When we are looking at the organization we need to ask:

- Are there more than 150 people here?
- Is there a common myth/belief? Think organizational purpose.
- Are people feeling connected to one another?

- Importantly, does individual behaviour match what is being said?

Asking these questions and exploring the size, purpose, connection and behaviour will help internal communicators (and leaders). These are the fundamentals to explore and when it comes to effective or influential internal communication. Ensuring alignment between behaviours and purpose is crucial to success.

Globalization and technology

The world of work is no longer always local. Organizations often operate globally with head offices located in one country and satellite offices in others. There might be two offices, there might be 100 but the use of technology in business has meant that organizations no longer need to be in one place. They can be connected no matter what.

Globalization has taken a few turns since the 2000s as technology continues to advance. Today we see a focus on making services global and personal, rather than the ability to ship things around the world.

I have grouped globalization and technology together because they work hand in hand – technology has played an instrumental role in the ability to operate globally. But technology isn't just about the ability to move goods around. It's about helping people communicate and it's about using technology to make organizations more efficient. In 2020, with the global pandemic, it was more than efficiency. It was about ensuring people were connected, felt part of a team and had the right tools to do their jobs from anywhere that was safe.

For organizations, globalization is about time zones, operations, laws, cultures and how it all comes together under one brand or organizational umbrella. Years ago, an organization was one building or one factory in one place. Now a lot of people can work from anywhere and the global economy has meant trading across borders is easier than ever before.

For those looking at communication, time zones are the question that often comes up. Internal events being hosted at a time to suit everyone, wherever they are in the world. Making sure emails from the CEO reach everyone at a fair time, and being able to collaborate and work together if you're in a team that is located all over the globe. Technology doesn't necessarily help here – because we have to remember that organizations are predominantly people, there is the human factor to consider alongside it.

Technology has to be better inside organizations for internal communication to be effective. Ways of working have to be explored to accommodate the time zones and cultures, and the traditional hierarchy approach to organizations probably needs a review if it isn't enabling the organization. All of this can be changed.

Not only does there need to be consideration for technology and time zones but also for the laws that exist in each country or state. The differences around what is required in terms of employee forums, employment law and holiday rights all contribute to the employee experience and all need to be considered with communication in mind.

For a global organization to thrive amidst all these pressures, communication has to be effective and influential. Out of sight and out of mind is not an excuse with technology in place but we have to look at team dynamics and organizational design based on tasks, not based on 'where someone should sit'.

The cultural focus for global organizations needs to be a core area for the internal communication function. With different countries, languages and customs being combined under one organizational purpose will bring challenges – it is the core of globalization and organizations. As culture and communication are intrinsically linked, globalization plays a key part in internal communication being effective and influential. Understanding globalization and its impact on how things work and how things get done must be considered.

Crisis and Covid-19

In 2020 things took a dramatic turn with Covid-19 impacting organizations worldwide. In many countries there were national lockdowns and strict rules around working from home as offices in cities closed their doors. For internal communicators this meant a shift in focus and a dramatic shift in the pace of work.

For organizations, the impact of Covid-19 meant they had to think differently about work. They had to explore what the culture really was inside the organization, what the working day really looked like and how to focus on people over everything else.

In lockdown and throughout the pandemic there was a big shift towards mental health, well-being and being human. Leadership teams across the globe were coming to the realization that organizations are people. Organizations had to pivot. They had to reconsider their purpose and they had to explore how they could shift their product or service and adapt.

Airbnb is a great example of an organization where the leadership focused on people and the focus of what it was there to do was addressed. The following excerpt from a letter from the CEO sent to employees on 5 May 2020 explains the changes they were going through and how they were focusing on their core business and their people (Airbnb, 2020):

> This crisis has sharpened our focus to get back to our roots, back to the basics, back to what is truly special about Airbnb.
>
> This means that we will need to reduce our investment in activities that do not directly support the core of our host community. We are pausing our efforts in Transportation and Airbnb Studios, and we have to scale back our investments in Hotels and Lux.

Not only has the impact of Covid-19 meant a bigger focus on people, it has also accelerated the use of technology inside organizations. The introduction of digital tools to help teams collaborate was taking years to launch – in 2020 teams did this in a matter of days. Zoom, the virtual meeting platform, grew from 659,000 users to reach 13 million users. The growth for some organizations was huge, as they strived to ensure people and teams were connected as everyone worked from their homes.

As organizations begin to return to site the need for technology in the workplace to support hybrid working has never been more important. The impact of Covid-19 will be felt in workplaces all over the world for years to come. Some organizations won't survive and some will thrive – some will adapt and some will start as a result of the pandemic. Speculation today suggests that the workplace has changed forever, especially in core areas like flexibility, employee expectations, how we learn at work and the shift in focus from efficiency to resilience.

Generations in the workplace

Over the last decade there has been a lot of discussion about the different generations in the workplace. With the generation who grew up with technology now at work, alongside a generation who have been working since before there was the internet, there is a lot of debate about the impact this will have.

There has been little research in the topic and in 2012, for an academic research project, I explored how organizations need to adapt to generational differences. This focused on Generation Y and Generation Z and how they communicate outside of work, to see if there are any patterns that could translate into the workplace. For clarity:

- Generation X are those who were born between 1966 and 1980;
- Generation Y were born between the early 1980s and the mid-1990s. They began to enter the workplace in 2004 and are also known as Millennials;
- Generation Z were born between the mid-1990s and 2010 and they began to enter the workplace around 2014.

The theory of generations states that people are significantly influenced by events that happen in their youth and that these events shape their future. A generation is defined by Mannheim (1923) as a 'group of individuals of similar ages whose members have experienced a noteworthy historical event within a set period of time'.

The opposing view states that vast differences can occur depending on culture and sociological factors and some believe that generational stereotypes are just that: some differences stand out and there are some similarities, but there's little to group them by generation.

If we are to accept generational thinking as a theory, we assume people born over a 20-year period are fundamentally different people from other age groups. We also have to assume that the similarities between them are strong enough to group them together as one.

These assumptions are vast, considering the population in each generation and their differing countries, cultures, beliefs and values. We also need to consider that historical events have different impacts on different countries and cultures depending on what they are and where they happen. Nonetheless, the role of generations in the workplace is a topic that communicators and business leaders need to be aware of. For internal communicators, understanding the different generations is important when it comes to technology and the changes that have happened during their time growing up. While it is a sweeping generalization, there is an impact for communication professionals as they look to engage employees on digital channels that fundamentally change the way work gets done.

Moving employees from printed magazines to receiving news in an app that they download to their phone is a big shift. And for those who grew up with technology at their fingertips this change could come easier than others.

Generation Y – traits

When considering Generation Y, Howe and Strauss (2000) identified seven traits:

1 special;
2 sheltered;
3 confident;
4 team-oriented;
5 conventional;
6 pressured;
7 achieving.

Generation Y tend to believe hard work and integrity aren't necessarily the quickest routes to financial success and have spent a childhood stimulated by television and computer games.

Author Simon Sinek questions the assumption that Generation Y are tough to manage and entitled. He believes there are four missing pieces that drive their behaviour:

1 Parenting styles: having been told they're special and can have anything in childhood creates low self-esteem in the workplace when they discover that's not always the case.

2 Technology: addiction to the dopamine hit that comes from checking phones and social media makes it harder for Generation Y to form deeper relationships at work and develop coping mechanisms to deal with problems.

3 Impatience: the world of instant gratification – buy now on Amazon, binge now on Netflix – isn't necessarily mirrored when it comes to job satisfaction or building relationships; there's no app for that.

4 Environment: taking all these elements into account, Sinek feels the corporate environment is too focused on short-term gain, rather than helping to teach Generation Y about cooperation, overcoming digital challenges, the joy of fulfilment and that it sometimes takes time. He believes leaders need to help Generation Y develop these skills.

Generation Y are more likely to have an entrepreneurial spirit: 'A generation that has been described as lazy, narcissistic, entitled, and unable to stay in one job, has also been described as the most purpose driven and potentially the most entrepreneurial of all previous generations.' (Daykin, 2018). It seems that the vast majority of Generation Y (84 per cent) say helping to make a positive difference in the world is more important than recognition at work.

When you consider this with our understanding of community and as we go on to understand people in more detail, these traits are simply some of the most basic human traits we have – and are nothing to do with technology.

Generation Z – traits

Generation Z characteristics in the workplace include challenging the traditional hierarchy-seeking collaboration, feedback and value from their work. They've grown up with boundless interests and in a hyper-connected, on-demand culture. They're interested in customization, social good and self-educating. They are used to working across multiple screens and have an attention span of 8 seconds, compared to 12 seconds for Generation Y.

There appears to be a shift between Generation Z and previous generations in terms of their unique value system. They see diversity as an asset and would like to see more diversity in advertising. They expect brands to contribute to society and this impacts shopping habits. They require brands to be transparent, ethical and responsible in all aspects of their business.

Although there are differences, there are some shared traits between Generations Y and Z.

Generation Y – communication channel preferences

A pilot study in 2010 explored the media preferences of Generation Y:

- Social networking is preferred less than intranet news but is preferred over the employee magazine.
- Generation Y demonstrate a clear correlation between content and channel.
- Traditional channels like face-to-face meetings are preferred for discussing strategy.
- For general information, emails and newsletters are acceptable.
- Mass communication and social media go hand in hand and are appropriate for most internal communication messages.
- The concept of the Semantic Web – which takes associated data (content, links and transactions between people and computers) and processes it automatically – with tailored and individual messages is not deemed necessary for internal communications.

- There is a need to consider individuals' social media use inside and outside the organization. Facebook remains the most used platform for Generation Y (74%).

Generation Z – communication channel preferences

Research (Field, 2014) found that Generation Z:

- See social platforms as a must; they spend their time on Instagram (73%), Snapchat (63%) and YouTube (62%).
- Are proficient with and dependent on technology to interact, play and learn.
- Are adept media multitaskers.
- Are more socially responsible.
- Have more access to the world through different communication channels.

While these areas of research help identify where Generation Y and Generation Z socialize and communicate, they don't explore how this links to their behaviour inside an organization.

My independent research, carried out in 2012, explored channels and messages to understand how the Generation Y and Z workforce want information, when they want it and who they want it from.

Understanding current workforce preferences allows for a more robust understanding of the differences in the generations. In the survey, 83 per cent of respondents in the current workforce were either Generation X or Generation Y.

Generation X and Y – the current workforce

- For the internal communicator, the 'journey for the business' is where engagement can be found:
  - They are most interested in the company's plans (80%) and plans for their own areas of the business (75%).
  - There is a strong focus on the future rather than the more static content like values and strategy (39% and 47% respectively).

- Different communication channels work together to provide a rounded mix; preferences show online and face-to-face are important, alongside recognition platforms as communication channels:
  - When asked what tools were most helpful, the preference in order was: messages from head of function, email, peer to peer recognition platform, messages from senior leaders and the annual conference.
  - Findings suggest that content around negative items needs to be dealt with differently from any other content to improve employee voice channels.

Generation Z – entering the workforce

- Email has been a topic for debate since Generation Z entered the workforce. While more socially adept, they're also very aware of the dangers and pitfalls of social media:
  - Over 67% would want information to be given to them via email.
  - Just over 45% wanted information via the intranet and 34% wanted it from their line manager.
  - Only 11% wanted a public-facing social media platform to be used; respondents don't want to receive information from a place where they create content.
- Having their voice heard is important; employee voice forums should continue:
  - Respondents would like to be heard through anonymous surveys (45%), followed by face-to-face small groups or emailing ideas to a dedicated recipient.
  - Just 22% wanted employee forums to be on an online space.
- When it comes to the most important things they want to know about, it's all about the money; pay (28%), followed by business performance (25%) and then learning and development opportunities (22%) were the top three items.
- Organization and individual engagement rated high; giving internal communicators an understanding that job and organizational engagement were equally important.
- They want to know it all; in terms of expectation, there is little they don't expect to be told.

- Who the information comes from is key and there's clear distinction between message and messenger; internal communicators must consider whether senior leaders or line managers share information. To fully understand this, there's a need to correlate the subject matter with the messenger.

- Social media and internal communications:

  - 78% of respondents expect to be able to use social media in their personal lives as they do now, without any issue.

  - Fewer than 42% expect the organization they work for to have rules in place around how the individual uses social media tools like Facebook and Twitter. Those who expected rules believed they would focus on avoiding any legal implications for the individual or the company.

- 'Always on' culture; just over 80% of the respondents expected the workplace to contact them on their personal mobile phone and 83% wouldn't mind if they did.

- Choice and customized comms; channels are determined by budget and business culture. The channel mix used is designed to meet the needs of the audience. The channels should be integrated so they work together. When asked whether they would expect to opt in or opt out of channels like they do in their personal lives, over 80% said yes; they expect to select the channel most suitable to them, suggesting they expect to have several choices and for identical information to be available on all channels. This implies the decision needs to lie with the audience.

- Face-to-face still has its place; being social at work and networking is something Generation Z should be naturally good at:

  - Surprisingly, 53% would build their network through a mixture of online and face to face with only 13% opting for an online only option.

  - There is a strong desire for regular face-to-face contact; clearly illustrating that this generation want more face-to-face contact than previously thought.

The findings suggest there's little to be drawn from the generational differences when it comes to internal communication channels and tools. The engagement of both job and organization remains high for all generations with a need for news and information not only personal to the individual, but also to the future of the business they work in.

Transformation and pace

There are many books about leadership, teams and motivation. Alongside these there are many books about change and the impact it has on an organization.

Looking at the role of leadership in comparison to managing, there are a number of trends that continue to come up and this could be one of the biggest issues in organizations today. It's one of the biggest issues for communicators trying to create effective and influential strategies to support the organizations they work for.

When coaching a managing director who was conflicted about his next step, the conversation cemented this issue for me.

The MD was responsible for a division within an organization. They had grown the division significantly in terms of turnover, profit and people, and things were going well. The growth meant their role was changing as they looked to take over their boss's role. The challenge they were facing was that their boss was also a visionary leader and had set a clear vision that people were following and building. If they were to step into that role, what would they do? How would it be different? What would they be they bringing to it when it isn't their own vision that brings about change?

This isn't an issue. As I explained: You do not need to change the direction or the vision of the previous leader if you agree with that and have supported it. You might change how that happens, you might focus on different areas to grow and you will no doubt lead differently. But you don't have to rip up what was before you to succeed – you can still make it yours.

In a lot of organizations ambiguity is the norm, often due to a leadership need to continually change. Business leaders are often keen to grow and take their businesses forward, so doing what they do really well and focusing on the basics is important. The risk is not connecting the 'how' to the purpose, and that is what leads to the issue of transformation and pace. The 'how you do what you say you're going to do' is important because it creates the culture and messaging for the communications function to work with. Having a purpose is so important but articulating how that manifests itself in reality is what internal communicators need to establish to influence stakeholders and build a sense of community.

So, if you are looking at your purpose or you're trying to work out what isn't aligning with the behaviours across the organizations, here are the five things to start with.

The purpose must be both individual and organizational

Take the time to understand what makes your people tick. It will be aligned to your organization and if it isn't, it gives you a chance to understand what is important to your teams – usually it can play a role in the focus for the organization as well. For example, a leadership workshop might unearth that saving the planet is a big piece of someone's purpose. This might have been missed in the company strategy and in conversation it might be important to everyone – and therefore you can change the strategy to reflect it.

The purpose is the hardest part

It really is. It takes a lot of thinking, conversation, sometimes uncomfortable discussion, but it is all worth it. Use a space that isn't in the office and give people the freedom to walk, think, take the time to work out what feels right. It's a creative process that can often feel uncomfortable but persevere and the rest comes easily.

You have to follow purpose with how

There is little point in creating a purpose without exploring how it will be fulfilled – whether that is values or behaviours. Look at the stakeholders and how this plays out with each of them and talk about the day to day. How does it impact your communication style with different stakeholders? What does it mean for the physical space?

You don't need all the answers at the top

There are still a lot of organizations that look up. Look to the top for guidance on what to do and how to behave. So many teams talk about not being listened to and so many organizations seem to have forgotten what they are there to do. Someone once said 'Decisions are made by those with the most to gain' but decisions should be made by those with the best insight.

Have the conversation in person

It's easy to think that you can discuss company purpose through a survey but this has to be done face to face. If you're a small business get the whole team together and run a workshop – if you're larger, work with the board and then the senior team to discuss and work through the detail.

Lead your team, your department or your organization with a clear vision and take them with you on that change with consistent, open communication. To lead is not to change so consider your leadership style and purpose and the impact it has on the teams around you.

Key points in this chapter

1 Organizations are people. They are not real things.

2 There are six suggested components to an organization; top management, middle management, operations, systems, support staff, culture.

3 Leadership does not mean there has to be change. Leadership is not about driving change through an organization.

4 You might see elements of Taylorism, servant leadership and others – it is important that leadership is genuine and demonstrates accountability.

5 Line managers need to make sure they are making time for people, asking for help and driving accountability through the organization.

6 Understanding the importance of emotion inside organizations is important when it comes to leadership. Employees want to follow a leader who is driving the organization forward.

7 There are six skills for leaders to master: compassion, looking after yourself, respect, time and attention management, self-awareness, listening.

8 Understand the community of your organization. Make sure you're clear on how it is growing, how it came to be and how things operate. You can do this through a variety of tools but understanding how it works is important when it comes to mapping communication to it.

9 A lot of organizations are global and with the introduction of technology, the world of internal communication has changed as workforces need to manage time zones.

10 When it comes to the generations, internal communicators need to review the role of social media and how they can integrate it with existing established channels, like email. Consider:

a **Customize internal communications**: information must be tailored to the individual and be relevant.

b **Use an intelligent channel mix**: review how the channel mix inside the organization works if Generation Z expect to be able to opt in and opt out of channels, while maintaining face-to-face communication.

c **Avoid stereotypes**: generations as a group of people don't necessarily have similar expectations, so this thinking should be avoided; there are too many variables that need to be considered.

d **Be dynamic with digital**: explore the use of social media and enterprise social networks, how it works as a space for employees to share information and ways in which it can integrate with your intranet. Collaborative platforms inside an organization and the platform where messages are 'pushed' should be different.

11 How we communicate in the workplace matters. There are some general traits, but we must remember that everyone is different.

Future internal communications professionals must continue to be dynamic – working across multi-channel – and be prepared to listen and collaborate with the entire workforce.

12 Have clarity on the 'why' of your organization and the purpose of it. Spend time as a leadership team or with the leadership team to be clear about what this is and importantly, how it will happen.

13 Be clear on the role and purpose of change inside the organization, and define whether it is really needed and what it looks like for you.

Quick tips

- Get to know your organization – make sure you know how it is owned (public, private, third sector, etc). Is it a global business or a local business, what processes are in place to get products or services to customers, etc?

- Identify the leadership style your organization has and the impact this has on culture.

- Look at the demographics inside your organization to explore generations and different factors that could enable you to group employees.

- Define the purpose and match behaviours and how that purpose is demonstrated.

References and further reading

Airbnb (2020) A message from Co-Founder and CEO Brian Chesky, https://news.airbnb.com/a-message-from-co-founder-and-ceo-brian-chesky/ (archived at https://perma.cc/YFN4-8UMJ)

Arruda, W (2020) 6 Ways Covid-19 will change the workplace forever, *Forbes*, 7 May, www.forbes.com/sites/williamarruda/2020/05/07/6-ways-covid-19-will-change-the-workplace-forever/#73266af6323e (archived at https://perma.cc/A7WZ-MTFD)

Baker, M (2020) 9 Future of work trends post-Covid-19, Gartner, 8 June, www.gartner.com/smarterwithgartner/9-future-of-work-trends-post-covid-19/ (archived at https://perma.cc/2MT7-9662)

Bolin, G and Skogerbø, E (2013) Age, generation and the media, *Northern Lights*, **11**

Borges Gouveia, L and Simões, L (2008) Targeting the millennial generation, *Jornadas de Publicidade e Comunicação*

Buchanan, D A and Huczynski, A (1997) *Organizational behaviour an introductory text*, Prentice-Hall, London

Crabbe, T (2015) *Busy: How to thrive in a world of too much*, Piatkus, London

Credence Research (2018) Enterprise social networks and online communities market size and forecast to 2026, www.credenceresearch.com/report/enterprise-social-networks-and-online-communities-market (archived at https://perma.cc/LTJ9-4W5N)

Crossman, D (2016) Simon Sinek on millennials in the workplace, YouTube, www.youtube.com/watch?v=hER0Qp6QJNU (archived at https://perma.cc/RCM6-WGUX)

Daykin, J (2018) The Millennial Entrepreneur, *Forbes*, https://forbes.com/sites/jordandaykin/2018/12/06/the-millennial-entrepreneur/?sh=c4ce09c7c40c (archived at https://perma.cc/NN5J-SZQD)

Deloitte United Kingdom (nd) Working during lockdown: The impact of Covid-19 on productivity and wellbeing, www2.deloitte.com/uk/en/pages/consulting/articles/working-during-lockdown-impact-of-covid-19-on-productivity-and-wellbeing.html (archived at https://perma.cc/T7RU-AA77)

DMI (2018) The changing customer: How to cater to gen Z, https://digitalmarketinginstitute.com/en-gb/blog/the-changing-customer-how-to-cater-to-gen-z (archived at https://perma.cc/H728-LMCD)

Dromey, J (2014) MacLeod and Clarke's Concept of Employee Engagement: An analysis based on the workplace employment relations study, http://archive.acas.org.uk/media/4029/MacLeod-and-Clarkes-Concept-of-Employee-Engagement-An-Analysis-based-on-the-Workplace-Employment-Relations-Study/pdf/08140-MacLeod-Clarkes-Concept-of-Employee-Engagement.pdf (archived at https://perma.cc/5937-YS8K)

Edelman (2020) 2020 Edelman Trust Barometer, www.edelman.com/trustbarometer (archived at https://perma.cc/9VUS-Y2JM)

Facebook IQ (nd) Gen Z: Getting to know the 'Me Is We' generation, https://www.facebook.com/business/news/insights/generation-z (archived at https://perma.cc/B7JW-A44F)

Field, J (2014) Exploring how Generation Y and Generation Z communicate and the impact this has on the future of internal communication, CIPR Internal Communications Diploma, PR Academy

Fontein, D (2018) Everything social marketers need to know about generation Z, Hootsuite, blog.hootsuite.com/generation-z-statistics-social-marketers/ (archived at https://perma.cc/6D8P-8Q3W)

Friedl, J and Tkalac Verčič, A (2011) Media preferences of digital natives' internal communication: A pilot study, *Public Relations Review*, 37 (1), pp 84–86

Grail Research (2011) Consumers of tomorrow: Insights and observations about generation Z, http://thsmarketing.weebly.com/uploads/1/3/4/2/13427817/excellent_generation_explanation.pdf (archived at https://perma.cc/FD69-H5BN)

Greenleaf Center for Servant Leadership (nd) Greenleaf Center for Servant Leadership, https://www.greenleaf.org/ (archived at https://perma.cc/6SBE-HFG6)

Harari, Y N (2015) *Sapiens: A brief history of humankind*, Penguin Random House, London

Hershatter, A and Epstein, M (2010) Milliennials and the world of work: An organisation and management perspective, *Journal of Business and Psychology*, 25 (2), pp 211–23

Howe, N and Strauss, W (2000) *Millennials Rising: The next great generation*, Vintage Books, New York

HRD (2020) How has the world of work changed since Covid-19? HRD, 1 July, www.hcamag.com/au/specialisation/employee-engagement/how-has-the-world-of-work-changed-since-covid-19/226597 (archived at https://perma.cc/LQK2-MDM7)

Kozinsky, S (2017) How generation Z is shaping the change in education, *Forbes*, 24 July, www.forbes.com/sites/sievakozinsky/2017/07/24/how-generation-z-is-shaping-the-change-in-education/#4746b52a6520 (archived at https://perma.cc/P6HM-3YCB)

Lawrence, K N (2017) *Your Oxygen Mask First: 17 habits to help high achievers survive & thrive in leadership & life*, Lioncrest Publishing, Austin, TX

Lexington Law (2020) Generation Z Spending Habits for 2020, Lexington Law, https://www.lexingtonlaw.com/blog/credit-cards/generation-z-spending-habits.html (archived at https://perma.cc/Z6E4-SFQ6)

Lunenburg, F C (2012) Organizational structure: Mintzberg's Framework, *International Journal of Scholarly, Academic, Intellectual Diversity*, 14 (1)

Mannheim, K (1952) 'The Problem of Generations', *Essays on the Sociology of Knowledge*, Routledge and Kegan Paul, London

Marketing Charts (2019) Why do different generations use social media?, www.marketingcharts.com/digital/social-media-110652 (archived at https://perma.cc/6PX9-AFKX)

Rampton, J (2020) How the coronavirus has changed the future of work, Entrepreneur, 2 June, www.entrepreneur.com/article/351157 (archived at https://perma.cc/4YQH-8LEF)

Redefining Communications (nd) Remotely interested?, https://remotelyinterested.work/ (archived at https://perma.cc/BR7N-7J7U)

Ruck, K (2012) Internal communication and employee engagement theories, in *Exploring Internal Communication*, ed K Ruck, Pearson Education, Harlow

Sinek, S (2011). *Start with Why: How great leaders inspire everyone to take action*, Penguin, London

Sinek, S and Yates, R (2017) Simon Sinek in conversation with Reggie Yates, Official Reggie Yates, https://www.reggieyates.com/news/article/in-conversation-with-simon-sinek (archived at https://perma.cc/VR7Z-QJJP)

Understanding people 04

We have covered the importance of understanding organizations and we touched on the fact that organizations exist because of people and assets. When we look at the history of humans, we know that *Homo sapiens* are the only humans able to create/comprehend myth and legend. We are not literal. We can talk about 'the majestic elephants', not just an elephant. We can make up stories and our imagination is incredibly powerful. We have created an entire legal system that doesn't physically exist – it's a set of rules and beliefs that we all abide by to enable us to operate as a society.

So when it comes to removing the chaos and ensuring communication supports the effectiveness of the organization, you have to understand people better. For communication to work effectively and influence others, you need to understand how people interpret messages, how they respond to change and the fundamentals of how things work inside our heads.

How our brains work

In 2019 the topic of neuroscience became incredibly prevalent for internal communicators – more agencies started hiring behavioural scientists and exploring the link between communication and human behaviour. With a better understanding of how our brains work comes a better understanding of each other.

We know that our brains are much the same as they were 50,000 years ago. Their primary function is to help us survive, predict threats and keep us safe. In the workplace, this means that our brains need to have clarity to predict. In a world of constant change (a faster pace than we have ever experienced before) clarity seems to be a commodity we are lacking. In recent years we have seen this manifest through worldwide events like Brexit and Covid-19. The lack of certainty about the implications of the Brexit decision and the complete unknown about Covid-19 have created a society in the UK that is in a constant feeling of threat – uncertainty has become so normal and the lack of ability to predict has impacted our ability to feel safe.

We also know that the brain has two halves – reason and feeling. The two do not often meet and this leads us to tricky situations. We can say that something doesn't feel right, but we can't articulate why. We can say that we don't like the look of a poster or a campaign that has been creatively designed but we can't suggest anything concrete to the designer to change. This is all because our brains are complex, and we underestimate them when it comes to communication and impact.

The brain has to be able to predict what's coming otherwise it can't keep us safe. To do that, a threat is the first thing the brain becomes aware of – it is almost actively looking for danger to make sure there isn't any. We see a threat before anything else – the threat and the risk will always take priority over anything positive or good. This is why, when an organization launches a new benefit for employees during redundancy processes, people ignore it. They are so focused on the threat of the redundancy and what it will mean for them that anything positive won't have any impact.

This is also why engagement campaigns need to be considered through a neuroscience lens. It's easy to miss the mark with a desire to engage people and in some cases it will lead to a revolving door of leavers. Imagine you're going through a TUPE process and you're moving into a new organization. This wasn't your choice and you have little understanding about the impact it will have on you and your peers. If the fundamentals around that process aren't happening (welcome from HR, payroll information, benefits detail, ways of working and expectations, an induction, IT systems access and equipment, a chance to ask questions, etc) people will feel threatened. It's always uncomfortable when leaders get excited about hosting big events or virtual launches for TUPE day when all the basics have been missed and people are feeling incredibly nervous, worried and threatened by what is coming.

Understanding why employees will focus on threat, how they will feel about the lack of safety in their organization helps us when it comes to influential communication. It helps to shape the words and tone for the message and it also means that conversations can take place around the importance of information – no matter what that information is.

Desire for information

We will always feel calmer when there isn't something making us feel threatened – when our brain can predict. The only way to do that is to have the information available to assess things – test results, job offers, etc – waiting for these leave us with anxious feelings and an inability to focus on other things. Once we know – even if the test results are bad or we didn't get the job – we feel better simply by knowing.

When it comes to people, we need to keep the following front of mind:

- Information elicits the reward chemicals in our brain. So telling people anything makes them feel better. Whether it is good or bad news, it's the news that makes the difference.

- If we cannot predict, we panic. This is because we want to feel safe. With panic comes threat, worry, anxiety and an 'unsafe' environment for work.

There are other factors that impact the brain that should be focused on when it comes to communication and the workplace; fairness, community, ambiguity, curiosity and novelty.

Fairness

Fairness is something we often gloss over inside organizations. But fairness is a huge issue for humans. We respond to the social pain of being treated unfairly in the same way we respond to physical pain.

This is important because this is not only triggered when we are treated unfairly, but also when others around us are.

If people don't feel they are treated fairly, giving them a new bonus scheme, a reward for something or some time off won't make a lot of difference. You have to address the fundamental issue of fairness before you move forward.

Community and social connection

It's impossible for human beings to have deep connections with any more than 15 people outside of their immediate family. This is Dunbar's theory and we explored this further in the previous chapter around organizations. When it comes to understanding people, knowing that we can sustain deep connections with only 15 people (not at once, in total) means we can understand more about connections in the workplace.

Humans need social connection to survive – it's important to us in part because our survival from birth relies on someone else caring for us. We have a permanent need to know someone cares. Tribes or communities are a huge part of this and organizations are made up of all sorts of these with functions, teams and locations.

As we get to know people better and understand them, the importance of social connection shouldn't be underestimated.

Ambiguity

As a communicator there is often a conversation around the need for clarity. This can be easily swept to the side as projects move along and people focus on the organizational outcome but in fact clarity is vital, for everyone. When we can't predict what is going to happen we feel threatened. When we ask for information and we don't get anything it leads to the breakdown of trust and then we remain in a threatened state until something changes.

Many people are told 'you just need to get comfortable with ambiguity'. This is impossible, we aren't designed to be comfortable with it. We have different levels of tolerance for ambiguity and while some will be more comfortable than others, we are wired to feel uncomfortable or threatened when we can't predict. It's where communication comes in and it's often the biggest issue for organizations today. For internal communication to be effective it needs to remove the ambiguity for the audience.

Curiosity and novelty

That need to predict can also play out in our curiosity and our need for novelty. We are curious in our nature. We often want to explore, travel, find out why something is happening – they are all part of our natural design and when it comes to the workplace this can often lead to others feeling uncomfortable with a person's interest in a project or offering to help – so just remember we are naturally curious and simply keen to help. Novelty is something that will often raise a smile. And when you combine these two, you can see why it is often hard to concentrate in open-plan offices. We are curious about what is happening around us and it is going to take more of my attention if I'm doing something 'boring' and what's happening over there is more novel.

We know this from research that tells us we switch focus every four minutes and that 44 per cent of interruptions are self-initiated. Being curious is in our nature but when you're trying to get someone's attention this is increasingly challenging.

It's also why new tools, changes to ways of working, etc see a spike in interest and engagement and then things start to slow down as the novelty wears off. Maintaining the interest of a human being in an increasingly noisy world is challenging. Communicators need to have the skills to make sure the content is relevant and engaging, and that the way it is shared is equally engaging and relevant – no easy task when you can have over 1,000 individuals working in an organization, all with different interest levels and requirements.

As communicators, there is often the task of engagement and this can often be linked to motivation. Campaigns to change behaviour or raise interest in specific areas is usually linked to motivation theory – and it's not as simple as carrots and sticks.

Motivation

'They just aren't doing what I need them to', 'I don't understand what's stopping them from doing what they need to', ' I asked them to do this list of things and nothing was done'. These all sound like very normal communication challenges. Why aren't people doing what I've asked them to do when I have been clear?

These are just some of the statements often heard from leaders of organizations or line managers looking to enhance team performance. Why aren't people doing what is needed? The answer is a combination of understanding what motivates people and then combining that with individual communication style.

There are a lot of academic articles, journals and books that talk about motivation. *Drive: The surprising truth about what motivates us* by Daniel Pink (2011) covers the extrinsic and intrinsic factors, and there are other, academic research papers that suggest amotivation (Deci and Ryan, 1985) is something organizations should be focusing on today.

So what is the difference between these and why is it important to understand them?

- **Extrinsic motivation:** There has to be a reward. The task won't be completed unless the individual can see there is something in it for them outside of the task itself.

- **Intrinsic motivation:** Where it's not about the reward. Pink suggests there are three elements: autonomy, mastery and purpose. You have control, you are doing the task to learn something and for the enjoyment of it, and it links to something bigger than just you.

- **Amotivation:** The individual doesn't want to do anything. They cannot link their actions and their activity to a result. It is similar to learned helplessness (Abramson, Seligman and Teasdale, 1978) and you will see it in employees who feel like they have no control over what happens – they will have a 'what's the point?' attitude.

When it comes to looking at a team of people and why they aren't doing what is being asked there will be a few reasons:

- Their intrinsic motivation factors are low. Have you given them autonomy? Real autonomy. Do they have a development plan in order to achieve mastery? Do they have a purpose or are they aligned to the broader team or organizational purpose?

- Are the basics in place? If we link to Maslow's Hierarchy of Needs where there is a basic need to have shelter, food, etc, we need to make sure these needs are met and then explore the motivating factors. If we don't pay people, they won't continue to work for free if it puts those needs in jeopardy.

- Is your communication clear? Remember the six foundations for impactful communication outlined in Chapter 1 – are you using them, demonstrating them and staying true to them?

The six foundations for impactful communication

1 Focus on the audience.

2 Set a clear goal.

3 Get the tone right.

4 Keep it simple.

5 Structure to make your point.

6 Adapt to the medium.

It's easy to focus on extrinsic motivation. Create a bonus strategy, pay scales, etc that support the theory. But there is a risk here. Daniel Pink (2011) noted seven flaws of taking a purely extrinsic approach:

1 They can extinguish intrinsic motivation.

2 They can diminish performance.

3 They can crush creativity.

4 They can crowd out good behaviour.

5 They can encourage cheating, shortcuts and unethical behaviour.

6 They become addictive.

7 They can foster short-term thinking.

Table 4.1 SPACES theory linked to neuroscience for organizational change

Self-esteem	Winning, feeling important relative to others, doing better than others, seniority, status, improving yourself, learning and developing, growing, mastering a skill, respected by others, sense of achievement, feeling valued and trusted
Purpose	Making a difference, having a sense of direction, having meaning, hope, feeling that your contribution is useful, helping others, feeling needed
Autonomy	Perception of having control over events or environment, free to determine how things are done, influence on decisions (even small ones), choice, not feeling constrained or micro-managed, feeling your voice will be heard
Certainty	Predicting the future, knowing what is going to happen and when, clarity about responsibility, knowing what is expected of you, short term goals
Equity	Perceiving exchanges to be fair, transparency, the process is fair (especially important during times of change), the outcome will be fair, being treated with honesty and decency, fair play
Social connection	Feeling connected to other people, feeling part of an 'ingroup', feeling safe with others, feeling someone has your interests at heart and is interested in you, belonging, inclusion

When it comes to communication this is important to be aware of. Extrinsic motivation used alone can lead to toxic behaviours, competitive cultures and siloed working. In an age where collaboration is needed inside organizations, and teamwork at all levels can be linked to performance, these flaws are worth noting and questioning for your own organization.

Hilary Scarlett, author of *Neuroscience for Organizational Change*, included her theory of SPACES for motivation: self-esteem, purpose, autonomy, certainty, equity and social connection (Table 4.1).

This table is incredibly helpful as you look at the team or organization. Everyone is different. For some people, social connection will be more important than purpose and for others clarity will rule over equity.

To help you with your teams and conversations you need to explore this. The way people behave will often give you an indication of what motivates them and some of the things in the table will have different weighting for different people – listening to individuals, watching how they respond to situations, etc, will help you identify the scale of each one for your team.

Trust and fear

These are two words that go hand in hand when it comes to communication. Research suggests that they are not only intrinsically linked, but that our ability to trust people or information comes from a foundation of fear and how our brains respond to it. In the workplace, this is so important when relationships with teams and leaders are required in order for the organization to operate.

Trust

In the workplace, and for internal communicators, the Edelman Trust Barometer has proved a helpful tool for tracking and exploring the role of trust in society and in the workplace. It has existed for over 19 years and it has tracked trust across the globe from NGOs to the media to peers to CEOs. When it comes to trust at work, the 2019 report suggests this is something we can no longer take for granted.

But why is trust so important when it comes to understanding people? Because it is fundamental to most relationships and therefore, fundamental to the connections of the teams inside the organization.

The study started in 2000 when NGOs were the most trusted in the world – and this has remained fairly constant. In 2006/2007 'a person like you' became a credible authority figure (and we saw the rise in peer-to-peer communication in the workplace where communicators used employees to carry messages across the organization), which shows lower confidence in government and CEOs. In 2008 we saw the destruction of trust in the business sector, and a rise of trust in government and then in 2011/2012 government trust dropped (linked to economic challenges, scandals in developing markets and more). Throughout all this time, the trust in media was slowly declining and in 2018 this reached crisis point with the battle for truth and the rise of fake news.

In 2019 trust became local. Partly due to the fake news and the challenges we have in the battle for truth, but also because it has shifted into an area we can control – our employer.

In 2018, fears about the future were spoken about as fear of immigration, and in 2019 the fear that mattered most was automation. Two-thirds of workers feared they were being replaced by machines. 'It is not an immigrant I fear, it is a robot'.

There is a desperate search for control, to take back power. As the decline in media had happened slowly over nine years, in 2019, for the first time, there had been an incredible rise in engagement with the media – from 50 per cent to 72 per cent in one year. We are deeply involved in the process of news and discussion.

During 2018 we witnessed more and more employees taking a stance against employers. We saw headlines of leaked memos, employees walking out to take a stand against culture or strategy. Employees made their voices heard and used technology to help amplify the message. They believe they have the ability to influence what is happening at work. And for me, they should absolutely believe this.

For CEOs this was the most important report for 2019. Seventy-five per cent of employees expected CEOs to act while governments were paralysed. Employees wanted retraining (due to the fear of the robot), they wanted equal pay (and more), and they wanted the CEO to have a voice in this conversation and stand up for what is right. There had never been a more important time to empower people to take part in the discussion. If you empower the people, they will be loyal, they will engage and they will advocate for the organization.

According to Richard Edelman, these are the four things CEOs need to do to obtain the trust of their employees:

- Have a big idea – an organization has to have a mission and a purpose.
- Inform your employees first not last – they should be ahead of your customers and shareholders.

- Focus on your home market – multinationals have got to make community work.
- CEOs need to stand up and speak out.

Internal communicators are the people to help organizations obtain trust in these ways. They understand the importance of leadership, purpose, employee engagement and community. There is a need to engage employees and reignite the trust inside organizations, not just through words, but through actions and behaviours at work that match. If we say we have an open-door policy and you can ask any question of the CEO – this has to be genuine to create trust.

Fear

Our brains are designed to focus more on the negative than the positive. We are hardwired to respond to fear as our brain's purpose is to keep us safe. While we understand the importance of threat and reward and the role of information, the role of fear for human beings is incredibly powerful.

President Roosevelt said 'Let me assert my firm belief that the only thing we have to fear is fear itself – nameless, unreasoning, unjustified terror which paralyses needed efforts to convert retreat into advance.'

This quote is so important when it comes to fear in the workplace because it's the fear of fear that stops us moving forward. We will often hear 'that's not how things are done here' or 'that's how it's always been' and these are born from fear. Something different, unknown will bring some sense of worry and it's much safer to stick to what we know, what we have always done.

Stepping out of that comfort zone is something we will cover later in the book as we explore leadership, but when it comes to fear – the power of it should not be underestimated.

When it comes to internal communication, employees need context for the information they are receiving. The regular updates on financial performance will mean nothing without an understanding of how the numbers compare to last year, or another metric – there must be context. Context is king here, especially as we need it to be able to assess risk properly.

There are two types of risk: relative and absolute. Relative risk is simply how much bigger or smaller a risk is relative to something else. Absolute risk is the probability of something happening.

Context is everything and in organizations the story that accompanies the information has to be combined with the risks so it reduces the worry and fear. We remember stories 30 per cent better than just facts. Add an image to that story that evokes an emotional response and you have got the brain totally engaged. This all sounds very positive but imagine the story isn't good, the image isn't nice and the overall context is challenging. The combination of all these elements together can create huge waves of fear and being mindful of that in communication is incredibly important.

We fear the unknown, and in many organizations that fear is change itself – the ambiguity that leads to feeling threatened can quickly become fear. And that fear gets worse with a herd mentality.

We need social connection because we are social animals. We are designed to be in a community and therefore to think about others. We want to know what people are up to, why they are doing it, etc, and this is all because it is linked to our survival. Cooperation helps us stay alive. It's why we have an innate need to help each other and it's partly why we prefer people who conform. It suggests unity, a tribe. It suggests we are working together and therefore we are safe – zero threat, zero fear.

Likewise, fear breeds fear. Much in the same way that calm breeds calm and the general principle that behaviour breeds behaviour. Herd mentality rules. Bring that into the organization and it will cause havoc if left unmanaged. If one person is scared that they will lose their job, others around them will become scared with little or no foundation for the reasons for the fear. The fear of another casts doubt in the minds of those around them. If they're scared, I should be scared – because it's about survival.

The more we can understand that survival is our core brain focus, the more we can understand the people in our organizations and why communication is so fundamental to organizational success.

The rumour mill has been around for a long time. As internal communicators, it is often an important part of the role to make sure information is 'myth-busted' so that people know the truth. But that of course relies on them trusting the leadership and the source of that 'truth'. If there is little trust in leadership, a big change programme and fear that is spreading throughout the organization, myth-busting becomes increasingly challenging.

Trust and fear work together. And when fear is spread through an organization, trying to quash it with facts and numbers and data won't work. Fear is a gut reaction, it's an emotional response. Numbers and logic are not. They don't really talk to each other and that's the challenge, especially in organizations where there are lots of employees based all over the place and relying on their local 'tribe' for information.

So how do you combat it? Time and relationships. We underestimate the value of this inside organizations. We rush from meeting to meeting without considering the people and our need for the story to be explained. How we work was a big focus during the Covid-19 pandemic. Our need to lead with empathy while in a state of fear was a huge focus for internal communicators who were battling with misinformation, unknowns and huge change inside organizations.

The core elements to moving forward, to 'convert retreat into advance' are:

- Leading with empathy in every conversation.
- Being genuine.
- Getting the basics right – making sure employees receive information before the public.
- Making sure the information shared is relevant for the audience.

The big one here is being genuine and as we cover leadership styles throughout the book this will come to the fore. Importantly, to be genuine also means you need to be vulnerable.

Vulnerability and bravery

We cannot be courageous without being vulnerable. Vulnerability without boundaries creates fear. These are two bold statements that are some of the biggest takeaways from reading the work of Dr Brené Brown, a vulnerability and shame researcher from the USA.

Brown is an international speaker, author and trainer who helps those in leadership take a more daring approach to what they do. This is a fine balance to tread and as we explore leadership in the next chapter, it's easy to see how this challenge plays out in organizations. Leaders are not taught to be vulnerable, and for the majority of organizations, leaders are men. Men who are conditioned to be tough, brave and show less emotion.

The role of vulnerability cannot be underestimated. We are trained to believe that vulnerability is a weakness and courage a strength but we have never looked at the two together. Knowing when to be vulnerable can be hard. Leaders can often be told to leave emotion at the door but we are all human. And vulnerability is one of the core ways to connect with others. Being able to show a genuine side and open up part of yourself as a human and not the label of CEO or operations manager will develop a deeper connection with those around you. Leaving emotion at the door? Definitely not. Having boundaries around that vulnerability to create connectedness? Absolutely.

When it comes to trust, and fear, connectedness is what will make the difference. Finding ways to connect with people as a leader or as a peer needs communication. Martin and Marks (2019) propose two types of messengers in their book *Messengers*, and when it comes to communication, the messenger is as important as the message (in some cases more so).

They suggest there are hard and soft messengers. Hard messengers have, or claim to have, a higher status than others. This may or may not be true, but you believe they have an elevated status and as a result they carry more power. These people are more dominant, are shown more respect and their traits include socio-economic position, competence, dominance and attractiveness.

The soft messengers lead with connectedness. They demonstrate traits of warmth, vulnerability, trustworthiness and charisma.

There is an interplay between these messenger types – a role for them across society and need for them in different situations. Importantly, connectedness through communication is what's needed when it comes to effective and influential internal communication. There are elements of both types at play, but underestimating the need for empathy and human connection is what leads to chaos inside organizations. As an internal communicator, exploring how you can bring empathy into your content is important. Make the human connection, bring reality to the conversation with honesty and explore how you can make connections across the organization.

Bravery

What does it mean to be brave? It's a word that is used a lot – sometimes to commend someone for having a voice when no one else will, standing up for something that is wrong, fighting for what is right. As a leader, being brave is not about fighting. It's about being ethically, morally sound and it's about being able to lean in to situations, conversations or events that require a deep breath and one foot forward.

Bravery is a word often used to describe those going into battle, taking risks and doing something incredible. We don't often use it in business or organizations because it is reserved for those doing more than standing up and giving a presentation to 100 people – but that is brave.

There are lots of ways to be brave and the work by Dr Brené Brown on bravery and vulnerability is definitely worth reading. Brown talks about the fact that you cannot be brave without being vulnerable – to have courage is to be vulnerable because you are putting yourself out there, and that's scary.

When it comes to work, we need to be vulnerable and courageous a lot of the time. We need to share our work for people to criticize, we need to have conversations that are difficult and we need to be brave.

If you've ever been coached then it's likely you would have worked through models linked to doing things you wouldn't normally do.

Doing things like taking that leap and being brave to try something different or have the courage to be the person you want to be.

But being brave in the workplace can take many forms and it can have many consequences. When you work with leadership teams, CEOs and strategic advisors it's easy for your voice to get quieter as theirs get louder. But if you don't have the courage to have the conversations you need to then you'll be working on things that aren't aligned to the organization and you'll be known as a busy fool – and no one wants that.

Sometimes being brave is about asking the right questions. Being asked again and again how your work adds value is a challenging question for a communicator. How does what you do add value? You can spend hours and days working through measurement and how to demonstrate the value you bring, ready for a board meeting where you need to present the value you have added to the year. You'll walk in, prepared and nervous, and share the statistics around the channels and the campaigns you have delivered in the year.

But you will have missed a vital step – a step that has to be taken in order to get this right. Ask the question 'What do you mean by value?' It can take a moment of courage and bravery to ask it, but you'll get the answer and ensure that how you present your value is linked to this answer – not your interpretation of the word 'value'. This is a real example and when this happened, the definition of value was around risk. So I reviewed, refreshed and reframed plans, objectives and outputs to ensure I was supporting the organization and managing the reputational risk.

It was a relief. The conversations switched from being about people to being about risk – the same outcome, but a different frame. Planning was easier – it was more focused. I wasn't distracted by other projects or ideas that could take me off course because I had clarity about what was needed.

All because I was brave enough to ask.

In Chapter 1, the value and impact of internal communication and the need for alignment was discussed. This is where bravery really comes in. If you're working in communication, align yourself to your leaders. As a leader, bravery will mean lots of different things. The courage to have difficult conversations or the recognition that you need to upskill in areas around communication.

We all need to be a little bit brave at different stages in work and life and recognizing the link to vulnerability is often the key to enabling the next step.

Tips for bravery:

- **You don't have to listen to everyone.** People will have an opinion about you, your approach and your work but you cannot please everyone. Your style, your way of doing things will be different to others' – there is no one way to be a CEO or a director.

- **Make a start.** Taking the first step, writing the first presentation, chairing your first meeting – we all start somewhere. You won't be like the person before you, and you don't have to be – you have to be you.

- **Be genuine/authentic – be you.** If you pretend then people will know and you cannot be brave without being vulnerable and to be vulnerable is to be you.

- **Take time to learn.** Communication skills aren't natural to everyone. Bravery can be the step being taken to recognize the need to develop and that's OK. It's a vulnerable place to be to admit you don't know how to do something and communication is a skill we can all do with learning more about.

Listening to others

Our desire to help others is innate. We are built to be part of communities, gossip and communicate. Listening to others is often something we struggle to do well. Because we want to help, we will often listen to respond, listen to offer guidance and listen to solve. Truly listening to someone means staying silent, focusing your attention on them and paying attention to the tone, pace, words used and body language (if in person).

There are lots of exercises you can do to explore your listening skills – work in pairs, where one person tells a story about their favourite holiday while the other person sits in silence. Reverse this and then discuss. You'll probably find that sitting totally silent is quite alien, but your memory of what they said and how that made you feel will be heightened.

Listening to employees became known as 'employee voice' in the early 2000s. It is a term used by many in internal communication, and very few outside the profession. Simplicity is key here, it's listening to employees and it doesn't need another name to complicate things.

Dr Kevin Ruck conducted research with fellow practitioners Howard Krais and Mike Pounsford in 2019 into the role of listening. Their small study identified four themes that get in the way of listening:

1 The way we define leadership – the way that leadership is understood to mean the 'need to provide answers' rather than involving listening to employees.

2 Under-investment in listening capability development – are leaders 'wilfully deaf'?

3 Cultural barriers – organizational cultures are not very conducive to listening and employees are often fearful of speaking out.

4 Structures and processes not developed to support listening – organizations do not always have a systemic approach to listening to employees.

These four points raise several questions about the way organizations operate but they also show a need to explore leadership. When it comes to influential and effective internal communication, it is easy to see how leadership plays such an important role. And if we still expect them to provide the answers then the need to listen to others will be diminished. By listening to others, we can really drive change forward.

In addition to these points, there is a fear that stops us from listening. We don't want to admit we are wrong – it's why we struggle to be vulnerable. Consider this with the culture inside the organization and how it copes with failure. If there is little acceptance of failure and a strong blame culture then listening to others, gathering feedback, changing direction will all be uncomfortable. It's easier not to do it. Head down, carry on and block out the noise. That's the easy answer – and the way your brain would prefer you to do things because listening to others and reflecting on your decision or approach is hard, and the brain wants an easy life!

As a leader, listening to others is about balance. Clarity around the reasons for listening is important. Much like a reason for a meeting is important – are people there to make decisions, advise on ideas and simply discuss? Why are you listening to them and what are you hoping to achieve from it?

Always ask 'If you're listening to your employees are you willing to act on the results of what they say?' It may sound like a silly question, but there have been too many surveys that ask employees about a working environment that cannot be changed – why ask when you can't do anything?

Equally, consider the purpose behind it and what you can really do with the feedback. During the Covid-19 crisis I was told about a leadership team calling all staff to check in. This was an amazing idea (each member of the leadership team did around 30 calls) and it meant that everyone was given the chance to share any concerns or issues. The caveat? It's unlikely employees will be honest if the CEO calls them randomly on a Thursday morning when they have never had any 1:1 interaction before. So, listen to them but know that they might not be totally honest, because they aren't going to be vulnerable at times of huge uncertainty, and they aren't going to be completely honest with someone they haven't built a relationship with, where there is little connectedness.

Tips for listening:

- Create the right environment to listen.
- Be clear about what you are looking to gain from listening – try to have something you are looking to prove or disprove.
- Make it normal – don't do it only in times of crisis.
- Bring the feedback into the organization strategy.
- Share the output and the actions within your existing communication channels.

Key points in this chapter

1 Our brains are designed to keep us safe and to do that they need to be able to predict. When things are ambiguous it makes prediction hard and the brain cannot keep you safe – that's where the panic can set in.

2 Fairness is a huge factor for human beings. Being treated unfairly or thinking that someone else is will have a really negative impact. Our desire for justice and punishment is linked to this hardwire in our brains.

3 We are naturally curious – don't be angry that the brain wanders and picks up on things that feel more interesting than what you are doing.

4 It's important to understand what motivates us. The old belief of financial rewards doesn't work so it's about looking at autonomy, mastery and purpose to help identify what drives people.

5 The SPACES model highlights what's important for motivation; self-esteem, purpose, autonomy, certainty, equity, social connection.

6 We need to better understand the correlation between trust and fear, and our inability to assess risks objectively given we are so governed by emotion.

7 There are two types of risk: relative (how much bigger it is compared to another) and absolute (the probability of it happening).

8 For the internal communicator, it is important to understand fear and the role of context in the communication that is being shared with employees. Having context reduces the fear of the risk.

9 Fear breeds fear and calm breeds calm – ultimately behaviour breeds behaviour.

10 Convert the fear and move forward by leading with empathy, being genuine, making sure employees receive information before the public and making sure information is relevant for the audience.

11 Understand that vulnerability and bravery go hand in hand. To show some aspect of vulnerability will make you a better communicator or messenger.

12 To create connectedness as a messenger demonstrate traits of warmth, vulnerability, trustworthiness and charisma.

13 Be brave by identifying who to listen to, take the leap, be genuine and take time to learn.

14 Take time to listen to employees – we don't do this enough in organizations and taking the time to listen, while being silent, can be incredibly powerful in unlocking difficult situations.

15 Create the right environment to listen, make it normal and don't only listen when there is a crisis, share the output with employees and make it a conversation.

Quick tips

- Remove ambiguity with information and provide context to reduce fear.
- Invest in yourself so you feel more comfortable being vulnerable.
- Lead with empathy in every conversation.
- Be genuine.
- Make sure the information shared is relevant for the audience.
- Take the time to get to know people in your team and organization to understand them better.
- You don't have to listen to everyone around you – find those who are best to give you advice, those you trust and those who will be constructive.
- Encourage conversation and be curious to find out why things are happening – it's OK to ask questions.

References

Abramson, L Y, Seligman, M E, and Teasdale, J D (1978) Learned helplessness in humans: Critique and reformulation, *Journal of Abnormal Psychology*, 87(1)

Brown, B (2018) *Dare to Lead: Brave work. Tough conversations. Whole hearts*, Ebury Publishing, London

Crabbe, T (2015) *Busy: How to thrive in a world of too much*, Piatkus, London

Deci and Ryan (1985) cited by Pink, D H (2018) *DRIVE: The surprising truth about what motivates us*, Canongate Books

Edelman (2019) 2019 Edelman Trust Barometer Global Report, www.edelman.com/trustbarometer (archived at https://perma.cc/9VUS-Y2JM)

Gardner, D (2008) *The Science of Fear: Why we fear the things we shouldn't – and put ourselves in greater danger*, Dutton Books, New York

Harari, Y N (2015) *Sapiens: A brief history of humankind*, Penguin Random House, London

Martin, S J and Marks, J (2019) *Messengers: who we listen to, who we don't, and why*, Random House, London

Pink, D H (2011) *Drive: The surprising truth about what motivates us*, Canongate Books, Edinburgh

Ruck, K, Pounsford, M and Krais, H (2020) Who's Listening? Good listening practice, https://pracademy.co.uk/insights/whos-listening/ (archived at https://perma.cc/FFZ9-VDBC)

Scarlett, H (2016) *Neuroscience for Organizational Change: An evidence-based practical guide to managing change*, Kogan Page, London

The White House (2017) Franklin D. Roosevelt, www.whitehouse.gov/about-the-white-house/presidents/franklin-d-roosevelt/ (archived at https://perma.cc/C7EH-8YX5)

Wikipedia (2020) First inauguration of Franklin D. Roosevelt, https://en.wikipedia.org/wiki/First_inauguration_of_Franklin_D._Roosevelt (archived at https://perma.cc/P56R-WW6R).

PART TWO
Applying the model

The Field Model 05

How to go from chaos to calm in your organization

Understanding organizations, internal communication and people are the first steps to being able to master influential communication inside your organization. We have discussed these in detail so that there is a clear understanding around the need to invest in communication inside the organization. As we explored the role of chaos and the damage of toxic chaos inside organizations, we can now see that there is a need to look more closely at the investment of communication in the organization.

Chaos theory is interesting because it is based around the unpredictability of systems. The world of work is unpredictable at times – the systems that we operate in can make things hard to foresee. As a result, chaos can happen. We now know how to bring balance to that chaos but what is also important is our response to it.

As communicators or business leaders we can choose how to respond to the chaos around us. Having the tools to respond calmly ensures that we focus on listening, understanding and taking action. We are looking to make sense of the chaos and using our naturally curious nature to explore what is going on behind the scenes.

The Field Model came from a conversation about how I describe what I do. Over the years the need to be mindful, explore other perspectives and manage emotional reactions has led to better conversations and quicker problem solving. When I describe what I do, I don't describe the activities, I describe the fact that I can bring calm to the chaos inside the organization.

The calm comes from a place of curiousness. A belief that more is going on behind the scenes and a desire to understand. The Field

Model is simply about codifying what happens naturally when you start to explore why things are happening. The curiosity will lead to questions being asked and, from experience, being able to home in on the blockers to success will enable change.

We can often get stuck without knowing why.

'I don't want to do that' is sometimes a phrase heard but this has to be responded to with the question 'Why?' and even then, the answer can be hard to articulate because the reason for not wanting to do something is often a feeling – not something that is easily put into words. So, we have to delve into the blocker: 'You don't want to do it because you don't know why you're being asked to do it. Gather more information and then you can make an informed decision.' Sometimes we stop ourselves from asking the questions and we leave meetings or conversations annoyed that we didn't speak up, or just disagreeing with points made after the meeting with peers.

The model was partly inspired by the need to address the short-termism that often exists for organizations and the quick fixes that come with it. It's important to explore why problems develop. Talk to people, find out what's really going on to cause a behaviour or a lack of engagement. Start there because the solution is not going to be a quick fix.

While short-termism is a challenge, there are sometimes cases where leaders and organizations are looking too far ahead. It's a fine balance to strike and the best advice is to focus on 30-, 60- and 90-day plans. The Field Model supports this with recommendations, known as the fix, that are designed to focus on things within this sort of time frame.

In this chapter we will work through the three stages of the Field Model. Communication is at the core because the model is designed to delve into the issues inside organizations that stem from poor communication choices and skills.

It's easy to tick a box and put a poster up. It's easy to say that something exists on an intranet and it's all too common to hear that managers don't have time to support their teams. All of this could be better if we take the time to understand what's happening and importantly why it is happening.

Explain the model, drawing a parallel with medicine is a great analogy. With the introduction of over-the-counter medicines we can treat symptoms like a headache or a sore throat very quickly. It's a brilliant innovation and is a booming market. And it's easy. A headache is an inconvenience and stops me doing what I need to do so taking a paracetamol is quick and solves the issue.

But it might only solve the issue for a few hours. And then I have to take the paracetamol again. This time, it has worked for a bit longer and I'm headache free for a few days and then it comes back, so I take the paracetamol again, and so on.

At no point did I stop and think what could be causing the headache. It was inconvenient, and it's quick and easy to take the paracetamol and carry on.

Had I stopped to think about the cause, would I have taken the paracetamol or done something else? Maybe the prescription for my glasses needs to be reviewed and that's causing the headache. Maybe I haven't been drinking enough water. Maybe I'm tired and I've been looking at the screen for too long – the list could go on.

Had I thought about the cause, I might not have taken the paracetamol. I might have booked an appointment at the optician, or had a large glass of water, or I might have taken some time to lie down quietly.

The treatment differs depending on the cause for the headache or the symptom. Trying to treat it with the same surface-level fix every time won't solve an underlying issue.

Apply that theory to organizations, and the headache could be any number of things – people off with stress, poor retention, struggles with recruitment – it could go on. It's easy to treat some of those with a well-being campaign or a new development programme to encourage people to stay but without understanding the cause, diagnosing why they are happening, the treatment will only create a short-term solution.

The challenge is that the people coming up with the solution are tricked into thinking it's working because their brains are signalling reward for doing something. Something is happening to combat the issue – great! People work hard on the creative, the messaging and a campaign is launched. It might be measured in terms of reach or in terms of impact and it might work. But what if the reason for the issue can't be solved by a campaign because it's actually about people being able to manage better and it needs a development programme to be created? But no one thought of this because – why would you? You have the reward chemical in your brain telling you it's helping and so you carry on. And while you carry on, the real issue gets worse. We have to take the time to understand what's going on. To diagnose the cause and then fix it.

Overview of the model

The first thing to mention is that the model is not finite. You don't work through each stage, wash your hands and you're done. There might be different reasons for using the model inside your organization and what it uncovers might lead to the need for further insight. In the next chapter on data and diagnostics we will explore why measurement shouldn't be a one-off exercise.

There are three elements to the model: Understand – Diagnose – Fix. We have to understand there is a problem, diagnose why and fix it (Figure 5.1).

The reason we talk about people, organizations, chaos and internal communication before we delve into the model is because they are the foundation to it all. This book is about using communication to make a difference inside the organization so understanding the principles and the theories around all of those elements is important.

While the model is the same for every organization and team, the output and outcomes are different. The way you fix things is different but there are usually themes that come up and in Chapter 7 we will go through some of the main ones. This will help you identify things in your own organization that might be contributing factors to chaos.

Understand

The first step of understanding the problem is the most important, and the most ambiguous part of the model. We can often fall into the

Figure 5.1 The Field Model

Understand

We often understand something is wrong. We might not know why but we know we need to do something. It might be because people are leaving, people are off with stress, there has been significant change in the organization through growth, M&A, crisis – whatever it is we know something isn't right. This is the first step – we understand the symptoms.

Diagnose

We have to diagnose the cause of the symptoms. There will be reasons for things not being right, people leaving, etc and we need to uncover what's really going on. If you fix the symptoms you won't be fixing things for the long term. Diagnosis can take many forms; from interviews to surveys – the right way to diagnose depends on your situation, organization and budget.

Fix

Now we can fix the real issues. This can take time – anything from a few months to a few years, but you are fixing the things that are at the root cause of the symptoms. Often, the fix is about refocusing your time and energy into a different place and we will give you a clear plan to take forward.

trap of wrapping understand and diagnose together, but in reality, we simply understand something isn't right and don't always diagnose the reasons why this is.

In some ways this is linked to our inability to articulate a feeling – sometimes things just don't feel right but we don't know why. So, we understand something is wrong. We can also often see things happening around us that we know aren't right. People going off with stress, decisions being made that are having a negative impact but aren't talked about, etc. These all fall into the understand category – because we don't know why things are happening. We work from assumption and this is when we merge diagnose with understand and think we have a solution.

Often, things go away for a while because the treatment of the symptom is working. This generally works for a maximum of two years, in organizations of any size. You can keep papering over those cracks and you can keep taking those painkillers but eventually something will give and you will need to start diagnosing what's wrong.

Two years might feel very specific but it's at this point that something happens to 'break the camel's back'. Whether it's too many people off sick with stress, people walking out or the business falling over – it's something big and it needs addressing now. While ideally we don't get to this point, if we can catch it here, we can fix it. But it's a long road to fix and we have to be realistic about that. The trick is to not get to the two-year point when things are so bad they are falling over. The main issue with getting to this point is the length of time it takes to fix, as it will take a minimum of 12 months to complete.

Understanding is the first step. Taking action when you understand comes next and that nudge into action is usually the hardest.

What does understand look like? It can be when something just isn't quite right, or when things have hit rock bottom. If it's when things aren't quite right, this might be:

- Lots of people are leaving.
- A business has been acquired and the functions need to align.
- External messaging isn't reflecting how people feel about working in the organization.

- Lots of people are going off sick.

- Two teams aren't getting on and help is needed to get them working better together.

- The business needs help telling its story and making sure people know how they fit in.

- I own my business and I want to sell it/step back and I can't.

- I want to grow my business and I don't know how to move forward.

- We have grown quickly but it's not working quite right.

These are the most common symptoms that suggest a path to chaos. You can see they vary. From the small business owner to the multinational, their reasons aren't the same and that's often because things just don't feel right – and making sense of that with words is really hard.

Being vulnerable and asking for help takes courage. As a communicator your role is to listen and ask questions to get into the detail. As a leader, you have taken the first step in asking for help from the experts around you. The detail is so important – the emotion that is being felt and the frustrations that the teams are going through. Listening and understanding every facet of the communication will help explore why there is a need to change.

Often, there isn't an answer to that feeling. Knowing you need help is the first step and not knowing how to fix it is normal – where do you go when you just don't know what is wrong? This is also why communication is often the solution. We communicate every day, all the time, so knowing that this is the cause of challenges is often the last place we look for a solution.

These are the checklist of questions to work through as you try to understand the symptoms the organization or leader is feeling:

- What made you pick up the phone?

- Are you publicly listed in any country?

- How long has your leadership team been in place?

- Where are your employees?

- How do you talk to everyone?

- Do you have any data about how employees feel about work?
- What are the core performance measures for the organization?
- Why do you think there is a problem? Gut feel or something more?

There are others but if you ask yourself these questions, what comes up? Do you know the answers? The questions are a mix of understanding the organization at a rapid pace and understanding people. This is the start of a journey, and getting insight quickly into people and the organization is the only way to move on to diagnosing things.

In this conversation you need to be listening and watching, listening to the language or the words used, the tone, body language (if on a video call or in person). Look at the environment of the office, pull in threads of thoughts linked to everything you have read in the first few chapters in this book. The micro-signs that come through the conversation are what to look for. Things that signal so much about relationships, how they feel and why they are worried.

Because they are worried. Things are chaotic. People are not having a great time. Financials are impacted. And they have asked for help. Step 1 is complete and now we can walk together on that path to change.

Diagnose

Now you know there is a problem. You know that things are not going well so we need to diagnose *why that is*. This is about getting underneath the problem. It's about understanding why things are happening and looking at the root cause of what's going on. It's easy to listen to somebody saying that their salary isn't enough and they want to be paid more. But you have to ask the right questions to really understand what is making them feel this way. Quite often it's got nothing to do with the salary. The salary is simply the tangible thing that they can grab hold of that gives them something to talk about, but there are links here to intrinsic motivation. Always explore autonomy, mastery and purpose when there is talk of salary. It might be purely financial, but sometimes it is more about having autonomy and ownership of a project and feeling valued. This isn't about questioning everything someone says as we have to make sure we aren't making someone feel shame or blame – but we do need to have a conversation about why there is a problem or why they are feeling that way. And that conversation needs to be had with an open mind, not one that has the solution already thought through.

We know that there is a disconnect between head and heart, between what our gut reaction is and logic. There is a reason people are going off with stress, there is a reason things aren't working well between two teams and there is a reason you're not growing as quickly as you want to.

And you can find out why. And as we diagnose why, the method for diagnosing becomes just as important as the diagnosis itself.

There are lots of ways to diagnose against a set of symptoms. For many in the medical profession this can be done using many different tests.

In organizations, we have lots of 'tests' we can carry out. Choosing the right test to diagnose the issues is important. If things are really not going well and you send out a survey, it will tell your team that you're not really that interested. In the next chapter we look at the different diagnostic tools, why you would use one over another and the history of the employee engagement survey. All of which is important because we have become stuck on surveys as the solution to all insight needs.

Use the diagnosis tool to demonstrate the intent to fix. Just as the messenger is as important as the message, the way you choose to diagnose the issues says a lot.

But how do you diagnose? Interviews are always needed. The data from a survey will tell you some things but it won't tell you enough for a true diagnosis. This is where a lot of organizations get stuck, and the issues with this and the reasons why it's dangerous are explored in the next chapter as we delve into the fundamentals of data.

Diagnosing starts with listening. Listening for patterns in language and feelings. Patterns, processes or behaviours that are contributing to those feelings are important to find. They will be there, and the more interviews you do the more you will learn about patterns and what they signal.

The diagnosis takes time. And it's important that in this part of the model you are listening to understand, not to fix. The whole point is that the reasons for things happening is unknown so you have to do what you can to remove bias and see the patterns form from individuals.

Facilitation skills come in handy here – you are there to guide the respondent down the path to their destination but you have to help them get there. You are not guiding them to your own destination. An important distinction and when working internally from the communications function it's easy to slip into a destination that matches your budget or what you know other stakeholders might be looking for.

Whether it's surveys, interviews, focus groups, 1:1 sessions with leadership – there is a lot that can be done. Depending on time and budget there is always a way to diagnose what's really going on.

Fix

This is where you need to be comfortable getting uncomfortable. It will require aspects of vulnerability, bravery, courage and listening to others.

It's likely to feel personal; it's going to make you defensive and it's going to shine a light on things you have tried to avoid. It's a deep dive into parts of the team or organization that you have wanted to leave well alone, after all, they have been papered over for some time.

What does fix look like? How can communication cover it all?

Communication is the fundamental component, the golden thread, that runs through everything. It is representative of culture, it is the articulation of the strategy and it's what we need to function as a group or community. So yes, communication covers it all.

The fix part of the model, which we will explore in more detail in Chapter 7, goes into the detail around some of the consistent themes but there are other things that could also be explored to reduce the chaos:

- Upskilling the team or individual – usually in management and communication skills.
- Leadership style changes – matching behaviour to the words.
- Consistency and commitment – building trust.

- Culture – defining it and demonstrating it.
- Respect – links to trust and can manifest in disrespectful communication.
- Prioritization – weak strategies can lead to a lack of ability to prioritize and manage time.
- Organizational structure – impacts processes and how things get done, which in turn links to the flow of communication through an organization.

The fix will require an investment of time, a shift in focus to the difficult aspects of organizations that require thought and attention.

How do you fix? Depending on the issue there are a number of ways the fix takes place. A task force can be set up, or you can opt for an 'on-site fix', which requires someone from outside the organization to come in for a period of time to move it forward (or turn it upside down for a while).

Changing an organization or a team is hard. People will be upset, because this is change. This is dealing with things that haven't been dealt with before; often, behaviours that have been allowed to continue despite most people acknowledging they are not OK. The challenge is helping people accept that they have to change too.

Too often, people focus on those around them who need to change, or the processes that need to. They forget that they all work together. Relationships rely on people working together, learning how to be together and get things done, and that requires people to adapt and compromise.

Your role in change

I have heard conversations in the workplace that would never be acceptable at home. In the workplace we are working together and that is a relationship in itself. The fix will often focus on these before anything else.

But things won't be fixed if we don't look at ourselves too. It's that simple. And it's naïve to think that anything will be any different if we continue to do what we have always done. Why would it? The reason things are the way they are is not down to everyone else. We all have a part to play and we all have to be accountable for what that means.

We can say all the right things – my door is always open – but do our actions mirror those?

Someone asked for help because things didn't feel right. We found the reasons why, now let's get to work to make it better. If you think you are not part of that, you underestimated what's needed. It's why we have talked about vulnerability, bravery, courage, trust and fear. It's why we have focused on understanding people and how our brains work. It's why internal communication is part of PR – because it is all about relationships and inside an organization those relationships are imperative to success.

Because if we come full circle (and remember, the model isn't linear) then you have to be part of that circle.

This model might be about internal communication, but it is designed to help your organization be more effective. To help your leaders become more influential and to ensure your teams are more engaged. It links to organizational purpose and being genuine, and so much of what we have covered already plays out in the three phases.

Why the model is needed

Internal communication has existed for a long time. The employee magazines, posters, campaigns around health and safety – they have all been used in organizations for years to communicate with employees about what's happening.

Over the years, the needs of employees have changed. Leadership styles have evolved and the world of work has changed hugely. With technology and the number of knowledge workers exceeding 1 billion in the world of work (Roth, 2019), we are more global than ever before. Yet some of the basics around communication remain lacking inside organizations.

Managers remain promoted for their ability to complete a task, not their ability to lead, engage and communicate, and we struggle with accountability and decision making now more than ever.

With all of that in mind, we need to review how things can change. It's too easy to get stuck in the hamster wheel of the organization. It's too easy to let the boundaries slip, work long hours and become part of a toxic environment. Work shouldn't be a horrible thing to do or a horrible place to go, and helping people communicate better can only make organizations a better place to be.

As we work through the model we are shining a light on the things that have been in the dark. The more you start to explore a reason for something, the more reasons you uncover. Lifting up a rock can uncover all sorts of things and, often, more rocks to lift up!

Once you're fixing the chaos, you're uncovering more things and things get more subjective. The model helps you work systematically through the challenges and even though you'll uncover more during the fix phase, you will become more agile as you move forward.

It's about test and review. You might use a survey to identify that someone needs leadership skills training, but to test whether the training has had an impact, you are likely to use an interview with the team. The flexibility of this model and the practicality of it means you are agile and able to test and review during the fix phase.

To really diagnose what is going on, we have to remove assumption and comparison. We need to measure and gather data. And rather than think that what we get is the answer, we need to use that data to inform further testing or put something to trial. It is often continuous, and our error is thinking the initial answer is final.

When we measure other things inside the organization we are looking for the answer. We can be more specific; people are happy with the benefits. People like the leadership team. That's not what you're trying to find out with the model. You're trying to find the questions that need to be asked to get underneath it all. You're moving the conversation away from assumptions.

Alongside assumption is comparison. So, if people ask you why the model is needed, the answer is that it's about removing comparison from our decisions. We constantly compare – whether that is in business, personal lifestyle choices, business success – we are surrounded by comparison. There is often a request to benchmark data against the norm or the competition and decisions can often be made based on what the information tells you.

But comparison is dangerous. It can be helpful, but the context around it is so important. The need to explore what the comparison is really telling you is even more imperative.

The Field Model doesn't compare. It doesn't take the data about your organization or team and compare against another one. It's about what is happening inside your organization. Delving into the detail around why that is happening and then fixing things in a specific way. The fact that another organization might be seeing similar symptoms is irrelevant, because every organization and every team is different, because people are individual, and people make up organizations.

For a long time, we have tried to create a one size fits all approach to business. In some ways that's because professional services are looking to be more efficient and they can see trends in data that suggest things are all the same – and some things are. The Field Model as a framework would be the same for every organization, but the outcome and output different every time. It's just not possible to take a cookie cutter approach to helping diminish the chaos when the core component in organizations is people.

How it can help

This book has talked about chaos and bringing calm to organizations through effective and influential internal communication. Chaos will always have a place and you will never eradicate it completely. But you will be able to reduce ambiguity and some of the other aspects that lead to chaos, enabling more balance and control with freedom and trust.

The Field Model allows you to structure your thinking, your approach and your timescales to deal with the issues that will allow you to carry on running the organization. Things don't have to stop while this is carried out, but things will need to be agile and people will need to be open to the change.

The factor to consider as you embark on working through the model is time. This won't fix things in weeks or months. You are likely to have some quick wins, but it's also likely that you will be shifting people's behaviour and changing how things work, and all of that requires time.

It's easy to want things to happen quickly, because it will feel that things became chaotic quickly. But the reality is they didn't. The reality is that it took time before something made you ask for help. So, you can expect the recovery time to be similar.

The outcomes you can expect to see:

- Changes in employees. Some people will leave (sometimes because they need to and sometimes the change isn't the right fit for them) and some will move roles. This can often be the most uncomfortable aspect as it's about people.

- Changes to leadership behaviour. Embracing and changing how you work is hard, but change is often needed at the top, and adapting and shifting is often seen as a result.

- Business growth. The focus on the organization and what it wants to achieve through this process works out what's possible and what's stopping it. For some, it means that when opportunity knocks there is a chance to take it and move forward, and for others it will mean that efficiencies lead to growth in the bottom line

Longer term there will be changes in teamwork, a better understanding of the organization and why things happen. There will be clarity for those in the organization. While there is often more turbulence during the initial time frame of the fix as things shift, there is a long-term change that brings more stability and calm.

With teams going through this, the model can help them explore the time frames they expect and their comfort levels with change. This is a by-product of the process and it encourages conversations around careers, skills, emotional intelligence and more. There is an element of unlocking the organization that takes place, with a safety that allows for conversations that might never have happened.

There are other, more personal ways for individuals, which the model can help with. Whether that is improving relationships through better communication, or development of self and others in line with the need for mastery to motivate – the list will be different for everyone.

What's important is that it will change how the organization operates, and the people in it. Whether that's their behaviour or the individual's, it's change.

Key points in this chapter

1 We need to choose how we respond to chaos. By choosing to respond calmly we can focus on listening and understanding. We can use our natural curiosity to find out what is going on behind the scenes.

2 The Field Model is designed to address a short-term focus issue and codifies what happens when you start to explore why things are happening.

3 We are really good at treating the symptoms – with posters or quick-win campaigns that deal with an issue like people feeling stressed. What we aren't so good at is looking underneath this to find out why people are feeling stressed – the root cause of the issue.

4 In the same way we can treat a headache with a painkiller, we can treat the symptoms of chaos with something to paper over the real issue. If you delve into the cause of the headache, the treatment would be different. This is the same for organizations.

5 Diagnosing the core of the issue is fundamental to real change and a real shift from chaos to calm.

6 The Field Model has three component parts: understand, diagnose and fix. Understand the symptoms, diagnose the cause of those symptoms and create a fix to address them.

7 You really need a mixture of interviews and surveys to diagnose what is going on. A survey alone is unlikely to give you as much information as you need to properly diagnose the issues – this isn't a tick-box exercise so the investment in time is key.

8 Fixing issues can be done in a number of ways. There can be a dedicated team internally, a consultant on site to drive the changes through the organization, or it can be something for the leadership team to resolve and drive.

9 Focus on a plan that allows you to complete things in 30, 60 and 90 days. It allows for a better focus and stops things being too short or long term.

10 Culture and leadership are two of the core themes that will always come up in the diagnosis phase and the fix will always show ways to move this forward through upskilling and being more genuine as a leadership team/organization as a whole,

11 Organizational design can often also be a factor in exploring roles and responsibilities and assessing the skills in the team or organization.

12 We need the model to help managers become more accountable and to ensure the skills of the managers are not solely about the task and activity but that there is investment in skills around leadership and empathy.

13 The Field Model will change an organization. It will change the people in it – either their skills will change and they will develop, or they will leave. It will change leadership behaviours and it will be a tough journey for some in the team or in the organization.

14 Be prepared to look at every aspect – yourself, the organization, the team – everything.

Reference

Roth, C (2019) 2019: When we exceeded 1 billion knowledge workers, Gartner, 11 December, https://blogs.gartner.com/craig-roth/2019/12/11/2019-exceeded-1-billion-knowledge-workers/ (archived at https://perma.cc/HX9N-QP8M)

Data and diagnostics

06

The fundamentals to make sense of the challenges

Exploring the role of data and diagnostics for influential internal communication is often challenging. Those working in communication will often describe themselves as a words person rather than a numbers person but the need to explore data and what it can tell you is a skill that is increasingly needed. Leadership teams will look for business cases for investment and measurement, and as we talked about the value and impact of internal communication in Chapter 1, we need to be able to look at data and insight to do that.

When it comes to the Field Model, we are trying to diagnose what is really going on inside the organization and in this chapter we will explore the ways to do that and the things to look out for.

How to diagnose the problem

There are lots of ways to diagnose a problem. There are also lots of factors that can influence diagnosis. The Field Model isn't just diagnosing a problem with the organization's internal communication. It is looking at the different aspects of the organization and different elements that contribute to its success.

To truly diagnose what is causing chaos, you have to look at both communication and its impact. You have to ask questions that delve into the subconscious of the individuals and you have to use the right tools to do this so that bias is minimized.

Communication audits are hugely helpful. Exploring what people want to know and what they need to know, alongside how they want to find it out, will help build the foundations of a communication strategy and channel matrix. It will tell you where there are issues with communication in that moment and provide insight into the gaps in content that are needed to fulfil the organizational objectives.

It won't tell you much about people. Or about the plans for the organization, where it's come from, how it was formed and what blocks success.

Communication audits are the building blocks for the diagnosis – so if you have one, great! Keep doing it and checking in on its effectiveness. But as a stand-alone piece, it's not enough if you want to have effective and influential internal communication inside your organization.

We have already covered that the model is not linear. And that measurement is not the end of something – it simply tells you what to look for next. Communication is not linear either. The old-style models of a sender sending a message to the receiver and that being the end of it disappeared with the introduction of the internet and then social media.

Communication is cyclical, which means that how we diagnose the issues inside organizations has to be too. It's why I can criticize those who stick with the age-old employee survey as the only source of measurement around organizational health – it is not enough. There has to be conversation to truly diagnose what is *causing* the chaos.

For organizations, the reasons for choosing one method over another can often come down to budget but also comes down to knowing what is out there. Surveys have been around for a long time; the first ones created in ancient Egypt and Babylonian times.

The survey market is huge. Through a quick Google search I can find a list of nearly 100 different companies' offering employee engagement surveys for organizations. It's no wonder that the employee engagement survey is the usual tool for taking the temperature of the organization.

The employee survey was first seen in the 1920s and pioneered by J David Houser. Houser was the first person to develop a quantitative approach to the topic of employee attitudes. The work he completed for Sears in 1938 placed them at the epicentre of the human relations movement.

Companies were launched to offer attitude surveys for employees from then on. Today, there are no doubt thousands of organizations that provide these for different organizations around the world.

What this means is that the survey has become the go-to solution for research. Partly because it fuels our love of numbers or statistics that help us prove something but also because, sadly, they can be a bit of a tick-box exercise.

It's easy to do a survey, let the results sit on a dusty shelf and carry on while telling yourself you are listening to your employees. But there are many more specialized and effective tools available to organizations today.

Diagnostic tools

Diagnostic tools come in many forms. So, when it comes to using them, we have to think about the points we discussed in the first part of this book around people and organizations.

Some tests are right for some organizations, and some won't work. Sometimes the insight is needed quickly and sometimes it can be done over time. Geography also plays a role. But more so than ever, technology can overcome those barriers.

This guide (see Figure 6.1) gets a little more complicated when you map the employee numbers to the company rationale or the culture. The way you ask for the insight will say just as much as the insight tool you use. If people are going off on stress/sick leave, then an online survey won't cut it. It will feel faceless and like a tick-box exercise. You need the social connection – and you need to remember the need to understand people as the foundation.

Equally, if the people you are interviewing are vulnerable people, using technology to conduct the interviews won't work here either. There is a lot to consider when choosing the right tool. Start by taking the employee numbers and the reason for the research into account, and you'll be considering the two main factors.

Figure 6.1   General guide based on employee numbers

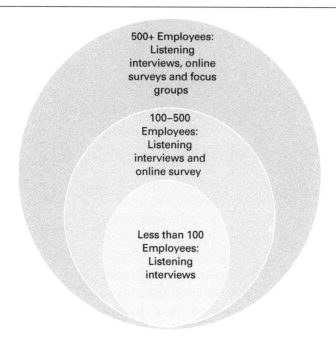

This chapter will outline what each method is, when it works and what to be mindful of so you can choose the right one for you. There will also be a section on other methods, like polls, that will help you consider other options as you look to diagnose what's going on inside your organization.

Listening interviews

What's important here is the language you use and your focus on listening. Anyone can interview someone, but a good interviewer is actively listening.

Active listening includes these key things:

- Eye contact.
- Taking notes.
- Mirroring the interviewee.
- Creating a safe space for the conversation.

- Paying close attention to the words, the tone and the body language.
- Delving into specific points made that aren't on the list of questions.

It's easy to work through a list of questions and make a note of the answers. But if you're actively listening, you're taking the person on a journey to help them work their way to the core of the issue. This isn't an easy skill to develop and it takes time to master. It's worth investing that time because then you're listening to understand, not just to respond.

If you have done any coaching courses or facilitator training some of this will be familiar. Just like facilitation, you're there to guide the interviewee down a path and reach the conclusion they need to, not the one you want them to.

Tips for conducting listening interviews:

- Interview from a random sample across the organization.
- Make sure you are completely present in the room.
- Record the interview or make notes – whatever is easier for you and whatever makes the interviewee feel comfortable.
- Build in time to have a break between conversations – they can be emotionally draining.
- Make sure the space for the conversation is quiet, comfortable and non-threatening.
- Pay attention to the language used, ask questions about why *that* word and delve into the emotion.

Watch outs

For many people this is a good opportunity to vent. If things are bad, they will welcome the chance to moan at someone and share all the things that are wrong with the organization. While this is helpful, it's important to note individual experiences don't make up the norm. Also, make sure your question set includes positive questions – what do you love about working here, who is your friend at work, what do you enjoy about coming to work?

Focus groups

I always recommend that these come *after* the online survey. I use them as a chance to discuss and validate the findings to sense check and delve into the detail a bit.

Tips for conducting focus groups:

- Keep the group to around 10 people.
- If you can, have two people facilitating the session to make sure you don't miss the feedback.
- Timings can be flexible, but two hours is the longest.
- Contract with the group how it is going to run, the outcomes you're looking for and how it will be captured.
- Give people something to choose between that gives them grounding – for example, if both of these items cost the same which one would you choose? This gives you better, more real data than just 'Which one do you prefer?'

Watch outs

Focus groups can be tricky. Be aware that people's gut reaction to things can't always be rationalized. As Dan Gardner says in his book *The Science of Fear*, you can put people together to review a car commercial and when you ask them how they feel about the car, someone might say 'I don't care for it'. When asked why not they might reply with a reason around the design of the car being ugly or a more powerful engine. This sounds like helpful insight, but it is not. The snap judgement that they don't like the car comes from the 'gut' side of the brain. The reason comes from the 'head' side of the brain – and they don't talk to each other. Being mindful and aware of this is important so consider the wording in the questions you use and look out for responses that could be coming from the gut.

Surveys

There are lots of different types of surveys you can do but there are three that I recommend based on the work with clients and the things they are trying to find out. There is of course the bespoke survey, but the three to consider are: employee engagement, internal communications audit and culture tracker:

- The employee engagement survey is designed to combine both general engagement factors and those directly relevant to the current organizational strategy.

- A communications audit survey provides the combined benefits of evidencing attitudes to both current communication impact and effectiveness. This provides the foundation for a data-driven approach to creating audience personas and segments, and pinpointing the ideal communications channel infrastructure and usage.

- The culture tracker is delivered through team leaders or organizational managers, with a question set focused on specific change objectives. Team members answer a few key questions, pinpointing strengths and opportunities for change within the team. The survey can be used on a quarterly, half-yearly or annual basis.

Watch outs

- Sometimes the data only shines a light on certain areas. If you ask about toothache but don't ask about a headache you're only going to know about the toothache and the headache will be missed. It's the same when we diagnose what's happening in organizations. Surveys can easily miss some of the key things that need to be discussed.

- Context is important. Asking people about the future of the organization in a year of growth and then a year later after redundancies will bring different answers. Both can be asked but making a note of what is going on inside the organization at the time is important. For internal communications we know from Chapter 1 that context and content is an important part of the strategy.

- Be mindful of sampling error. If you ask five people outside one office, you'll get answers from just those people. It might be better to ask people from different locations, or different levels in the organization. You might also need to make a conscious decision not to speak to people who are working through their notice period, etc. Consider the sampling and how it will work for you to achieve what you are looking for.

- You have to measure things with a reasonable frequency and consistency. As you're measuring attitudes to things, you're going to need data spread out over time to look at trends and make sure the data isn't skewed too much.

Surveys during crisis

In times of crisis it's also easy to stop any kind of data gathering, but that's not always the case. During the Covid-19 outbreak in 2020 this was a topic for many internal communicators. It's easy to stop measuring when there are things happening that could suggest it isn't the right time. But you should still survey:

- The choice is between measuring and not measuring, and in a crisis measurement and feedback are very important.
- While the overall numbers will be impacted by the overall situation, what you should be looking at in the data is relative scores (what areas have been impacted) and giving yourself a baseline for measurement post-crisis.
- It is critically important to understand, in a direct, unfiltered way, what your people are experiencing in the moment. It is also important to balance the 'direction' of communications, as there has likely been a large amount of outbound and little 'inbound' content.
- If you have switched working styles, this is a chance to check in on overall employee well-being and identify any interventions that might be required. Well-being should be a standard part of an employee engagement survey these days.
- If you're not already, you need to go digital (this isn't the time for sending paper around).
- One of the main things to consider is the speed of the action around the results. This isn't the time for the survey to be out for months and then weeks or months of analysis and creating action plans.

In terms of messaging – this will be specific for the organization but consider:

- Why you're doing it and why it's important to you – be clear about this upfront.
- Acknowledge that this is a difficult time for many but it's also why we need to know more about the well-being of our teams.
- This will be different from previous years as the results and actions will be out quicker and you are prioritizing actions to support employees.
- Expect a short-, mid- and long-term plan – and also some things that cannot be changed.
- Employee voice is important – and physical distance is no reason for it not to be heard.

You might feed back results in a variety of ways – ordinarily this might be on the intranet or in manager briefings. Why not consider a pre-recorded video update or a live video call to discuss the results with senior leaders? You could gather smaller groups across the organization to allow for conversation and get all the senior leaders involved.

Data collection is important even during a crisis. Continue to run it, create a baseline for the circumstances and be in a position to take quick action on the back of it.

Polls

Polls provide fast and effective feedback, while serving different purposes to long-form surveys, interviews and focus groups. Poll questions should always be informed and contextualized by these other types of feedback. Remember that context in information is hugely important, as we discussed in Chapter 3.

The poll questions themselves are as much a part of the communication process as the answers. What conclusions are users likely to draw from the questions and answers that they see? An important part of question design is making them part of the communications plan and avoiding unintended outcomes, as well as ensuring the maximum benefit from having polls. If you're launching a new digital platform in your organization effective polls can boost engagement and accelerate the adoption, so polls should be viewed as part of the adoption journey.

Establishing polls involves getting users familiar and comfortable with them, and baselining responses. Start with using polls to communicate and focus, rather than just gathering initial feedback. As an example:

- Did you know you can comment on content?
- Did you know you can share content with someone via email?
- Did you know you can subscribe to content?
- Did you know there is an HR portal?

Supporting the onboarding of users on new digital tools with questions about functionality like the list above is a good way to drive measurement and engagement. Ensure that initial questions are simple to answer, and aren't misinterpreted as an assessment of users' knowledge or capabilities.

Once polls are part of the communications cadence, they can then be used to sense opinions. Initial responses should be taken as a guide, until it is clear which groups of users are most likely to respond, and how. Once they are established, and potential response biases are understood, polls can be used alongside other insights to provide an additional source of measurement.

A regular cadence is important for poll questions, both to avoid response fatigue, and also to enable users to anticipate when poll questions will appear. Across all channels there should not be more than one per day, and ideally not more than once a week.

Poll questions can be used as a strategy to produce or stimulate content, for example the results of a poll may merit an article/post because the results are interesting, or because they indicate that clarification or additional communication is required.

Polls are best used for active listening. 'You said, we did' is just as important as it is in more extensive listening projects. Be sure to demonstrably act on poll results, where they are actionable, and to ensure that people are aware of the actions that have been taken. This feedback loop can even be incorporated into further poll questions:

'Were you aware of the face-to-face pension workshops taking place across the company?'

Remember that all polls are attitudinal, in that they measure what users think, within the bounds of what they believe it is acceptable to think! This means that they have different properties from other measurements, and that results should always be contextualized with other feedback. Grouping the results of multiple poll questions together can help to contextualize them for stakeholders and helps to focus on broader themes.

Combining diagnostic tools

Knowing which tool to use, and when to use it, comes with years of practice and an understanding of those who are taking part.

For example, when combining a survey with a listening interview, you need to consider the order of them and the questions you ask. If you are surveying employees and customers to understand how to change processes or ways of working, you would need to use different tools for each of these groups. Sometimes the access to technology is easy for employees but not for customers.

In this situation, you can run listening interviews with customers and conduct a survey combined with some listening interviews with employees. The employee questions could ask about the perception of the customer experience. The customer interviews could include rating scales on specifics in addition to the conversational questions. Combining these means you can measure the gap between the perception and reality as well as exploring ratings through interviews.

The method is tailored to the needs of the audience and the questions provide huge insight into the challenges that need to be addressed. Making sure the approach to the diagnosis is bespoke to the organization and the specific chaotic issues is hugely important. There is no 'one size fits all' approach, and where we try to do that, we suffer from results that don't help us to move forward.

The role of benchmarking and context

Benchmarking is a funny one when it comes to diagnosing what is going on inside an organization. It links to context and our need to compare – but it doesn't always help us.

As human beings we want/need to compare what we do with how others do it. This is partly because we want approval for what we are doing from our tribe/social circle but also because we want confirmation that what we are doing is right – it has some links back to accountability and how comfortable we are with making decisions.

I can run the same survey in two organizations. I will get different results and I can compare them but they will lack context. As we talk about bias later in this chapter we will discuss the challenge with context but here, the context is hugely valuable in telling the whole story.

There might be a query to benchmark video views – what's good? What's bad? What's normal? None of this is helpful. There is no 'normal' because there are too many variables between organizations, content and channels.

The Field Model diagnostic tests are not compared with other organizations because they are tailored. You should focus on diagnosing the issues that exist for your organization or team. Focus on the purpose of the organization, what's right for it, and then look at frequency and consistency to build the pattern. Comparative diagnostics don't help you, they simply move your focus away from your people and your purpose.

Data that matters

It's all about context. And it's about making sure that the data is relevant to what you're trying to achieve. You can label your organization as something and measure against that but is it really telling you anything? Data must have meaning in order for it to help communication. The data should inform strategy and messaging, so it has to be real.

You could ask people 'How bacon is this organization?' And people say, 'Well it's really bacony', or 'It's not very bacony'. Now you have a measure that says, 'We are 10 per cent more bacony than last month,' but it doesn't correlate to anything in the real world. This is clearly a made-up example but replace bacon with any other word organizations use to describe themselves and you can see how meaningless it can be.

We measure things that don't mean anything because sometimes people want numbers or data to make themselves feel better or to justify why they do what they do. But you don't need it. Digital dashboards measure all sorts of things but when you ask the question 'what do you do with this and why are you gathering it?' so often the answers are blank faces. It just makes us feel better to have something that says 'look, it's working' but what is working? What are you trying to achieve?

If we take the example of web pages and the need to show how many people visited a page, it often doesn't consider how many might be bots, or how many people have cached the page and therefore it won't count them – there are many ways where the data we gather tells the picture we want it to. And at the same time, we can easily get the data to tell the story we want to tell – and that's where we come to bias.

Bias and data go hand in hand. The case study in this section shows that, and when it comes to using data to better understand what is happening inside your organization, there will be bias in the question setting as well as the interpretation of it.

'Computer says no': data bias, algorithms and the Apple Card

When Apple launched the Apple Card in August 2019 it claimed to represent everything the company stands for: 'simplicity, transparency and privacy'. But it wasn't long before people noticed something strange. The card's issuer, Goldman Sachs, was giving lower credit limits to female applicants. Even Apple's co-founder, Steve Wozniak, remarked that he was offered ten times the credit of his wife, despite sharing all assets and accounts, and filing joint tax returns.

In an announcement, Goldman Sachs asserted that the algorithm didn't use gender as a criterion for decision making and that they were committed to making the application process non-gender-biased. If that was the case, critics questioned, what could be behind these seemingly biased outcomes?

Using data, machine learning and algorithms to support decision making is already well established. Whether it's for a credit card, loan, recruitment or to identify a suspect, there's an assumption that algorithms can take factual data and make complex judgements unaffected by emotion, stereotype or bias. This assumption is where the problem lies.

At the heart of the issue is that many stages of the data life cycle require human involvement. This means human bias gets translated into algorithms. Despite improved equality in many areas of society, everyone exhibits a degree of unconscious bias. Countless studies have found we all have a level of racial or gender bias that shape our unique views. These stereotypes develop from a young age and help us find our way in the world, but there's a potential for discrimination and negative typecasting. Algorithms are written based on human assumptions and therefore companies are at risk of automating unconscious bias.

In her book, *Weapons of Math Destruction*, mathematician Cathy O'Neil discusses the darker side of data. People view mathematics as neutral and correct, but the problem with algorithms is that they're based on models that are 'opinions embedded in mathematics'. O'Neil warns that algorithms are significantly affecting people's lives, since there is often no accountability or appeals procedure for the models used; 'By trusting the data that's actually picking up on past practices and by choosing the definition of success, how can we expect the algorithms to emerge unscathed?'

It's not just Apple that's been affected by this issue; algorithm bias has been called out in several other high-profile companies, including Amazon, Google, and Microsoft. Amazon's (now withdrawn) recruiting tool used CVs submitted over ten years to develop models that filtered applications by observing patterns in resumes. Unfortunately, the dominance of men in the technology industry meant that, through machine learning, any phrases associated with female applicants, such as 'member of the women's debating team' were discounted and this led to a reduction in female recruits.

Can machine learning remove bias, or is there a risk it could create more unfairness? In the case of the Apple Card, it's possible that the faulty algorithm centred on a 'proxy for gender' and applied it to credit limits, since there are gender differences in credit history. Algorithms use a combination of data points to make decisions; for example, it may have 'learnt' that people who also have credit cards at a specific women's retailer are a bad risk, or it may assess differences in income. This means that relating behaviours and lifestyle that correlate with women could have distorted the outcome of the application process.

Perhaps there are even inherent dangers in *not* taking gender or race into account: counter-intuitively, companies need to use gender or racial information to critically monitor whether their algorithms are introducing bias; to check they're built with impartiality and diversity of thought. Organizations need better decision-making frameworks with easy access to data insights. This also needs to be combined with careful definitions of success and measurement, learning mechanisms and independent evaluation to minimize bias.

As organizations increasingly use data and algorithms as a filtration system to support decision making, they must ensure they audit neutral data and create algorithms that exclude negative bias. As Steve Wozniak says, 'Algos obviously have flaws. A huge number of people would say, "We love our technology, but we are no longer in control." I think that's the case.'

This is about collecting data that matters. When we look at the organizations running large-scale employee engagement surveys and gathering data, they are usually doing it because they want to show they are doing a good job. With that awareness in mind, we should be mindful of the risk that we can consciously or subconsciously manipulate data to show what we want. If we are collecting data to show we are doing a good job or to demonstrate the need for a budget we are at risk of making sure it shows what we want it to.

The role of bias

There are different types of bias when it comes to data: sampling, collecting and interpreting. There are several layers that weave into these three aspects and it's important that we have awareness of them when we use diagnostic tools.

As an example, there will often come a time when people ask about incentivizing participation, but that leads to bias and it's an easy one to miss. People might only complete the survey because of the incentive, so their motivation for answering honestly and taking the time will be less than those who are there because they want to provide a response. While research suggests incentives don't have an impact on response rates, the quality of the responses is what needs to be considered.

Sampling and collecting bias

Who you choose to interview or who you choose to send a survey to will have a bias. If you choose to run a survey in person on a Friday afternoon in the office when you know 80 per cent of the workforce work from home that day – you have sampling bias.

If the email with the link to the survey only goes out to four distribution lists instead of all of them, you have a sampling bias.

This is the easiest one to avoid and the easiest one to catch but important to highlight.

How we collect the data will have bias, especially if it is incentivized. Incentivizing participation skews the data to those who want the incentive, not those who want to take part. So, if the incentive is a helium balloon and people want a helium balloon, they will take part. If they don't, they won't.

Incentives are different from rewards. You can be rewarded for taking part – the difference is subtle but I can reward you for taking part at the end of a survey and you're not expecting it – that won't create a bias because it's not linked to the motivation to complete the survey.

Interpreting bias

This is very tricky because there are lots of things that can come into play here. From individual bias based on past experiences, personal beliefs, etc, through to the context around the data gathering, there are lots of factors that can cause us to interpret data in a biased way. However, context is the number one consideration when interpreting data.

Equally there is a bias here that is linked to the group dynamics of an organization. This mirrors some of the understanding we have around people and how we respond to language or belief in words/

brands. If we believe our company can do no wrong, then as a group, that group-think bias will come into play.

There is also bias linked to the reasons for the data being collected and the behaviours that can come with that. If we run a diagnostic on the customer experience and we incentivize the staff to gather that data – it shifts behaviour and attitude. People might start giving better customer service because they are being rewarded for it, not because they are engaged or feel aligned to the company's purpose.

There are ways to mitigate against bias. It will always be present but here are some tips to help:

- Think about the language you're using. You don't want to 'lead the witness' so think about how the questions are phrased to ensure there isn't leading.

- Incentives and rewards are tricky – you don't want people to complete the survey because they have been incentivized to do so. The data you get will have a bias because of the motivation for completion.

- You can ask an independent person to review the results – this is really helpful for a communications team as it brings a review that isn't tainted by the organizational culture or previous relationships, etc.

- Make sure you consider when you're collecting the data – give people a realistic time frame and make it accessible to everyone – an inclusive survey is important.

Data

There are many ways you can gather data – polls, surveys, interviews, focus groups and more. Interpreting what you have, if you already have it, is equally important. It's also important to explore the questions you're using to make sure they will get you the right results.

What are you trying to achieve? What do you need to understand? Is it how people feel or is it about how people move box A to room C? Are you looking at people and process, or just one of those? Either way, the objectives for understanding are important.

Data can feel like a big word. Some have said they have enough data in their organization, they just don't know what to do with it. So, what do we mean by data and where does it come from?

The Oxford Dictionary definition of data is 'facts and statistics gathered together for reference or analysis'. The fact is, so much of what we do is based on assumption, and therefore we risk doing things without verifying them. Data is the solution to this problem.

Data is not just the information you can gather from surveys about how engaged people are. Data exists everywhere, and if you're looking to understand what is wrong, you need to understand the relevant parts of the organization that link to the chaos.

This means you'll start to look at:

- Process documentation.
- Software used to manage the everyday.
- How things get done – if you make widgets, how do they work their way through the organization and what happens on that journey? A hierarchy chart won't show you that.
- Financial reports, annual reports, investor information, government reporting.

To truly start the diagnosis, you need to understand data from every part of the organization.

You might be gathering data to understand process, not just how people feel. Data about how things happen. How you move one box from A to B or what people think about culture or communication. What's important is that you narrow the scope of what you're looking at. Don't try to cover too many things at once.

Aligning the objective and the data

To make sure that you're understanding the data properly, before you even begin you need to have a hypothesis that you're trying to prove or disprove.

The first thing to consider when it comes to data is the mental model you have of what's going on – is it the same as reality?

Benjamin Ellis, a data scientist, leading the way in the use of data in employee engagement surveys through his tool, SurveyOptic. He talks about the maps we have of the organizations we work for. One person's map of their organization's world might be different to another employee's map. If the maps are generally the same things will be OK, but if they are looking at two very different maps, then things will implode. The point of data is that it's meant to be an objective measure of reality. We so often use it in ways to persuade and influence and we move aspects of the data to fit the narrative we want to tell.

It is important to identify the objective of the collection of data – the kinds of data you are looking to gather and the hypothesis you want to prove or disprove. There will be one, even if it is simply about how people feel about working at the organization.

Quite often we get stuck measuring subjective things. Is this wine nice? The answer is completely subjective. This is the challenge organizations have when it comes to looking at things like engagement or the success of internal communication – they are completely subjective. My reality is different to your reality – it doesn't mean one is right and one is wrong, but we need to understand each other's to move forward together. Understanding each other and the data will mean we can find ways to shift the communication to be more influential and more effective.

Turning the subjective into the objective

In my interview with Benjamin, he explained how the use of the Likert scale has changed our understanding of the different types of data. Today, we think of data as numbers that paint a picture – 'we make 56 widgets a day' – and this statistic gives us a picture of the organization. The ability to paint a picture with numbers when it comes to feelings and individual perspectives needs more than simple statistics – and this is where the Likert scale came in, according to Benjamin:

> One of the geniuses of the invention of Likert scales was that it allowed you to quantify whether thousands of people like a thing or not. You don't really care

whether a specific individual likes it or not. What you want to know is, would the majority of people like this product? And so, the trick of a Likert scale, is it takes something that is subjective: 'I like this. I don't like this', and turns it into something objective. Because by saying 'strongly agree, strongly disagree' it will become one, two, three, four, five, you now have something you can do math on, so it becomes data. So, the Likert was a great invention around the time of mass computing that turns this fluffy people stuff into data.

Today, you can take this approach and apply it to all sorts of things to give you data – reasons why people leave, reasons they join, etc. You can even explore how long people spend in the office or when they take breaks, and that leads to understanding behaviour. Now you have data telling you what's going on inside the organization.

As we understand how we can turn behaviours into data we also need to make sure we understand that data is a reflection of what has happened. The data you gather will always be a lagging indicator. Knowing your staff turnover tells you they left but what you really want to know are the attitudes and opinions that would enable you to prevent it. If somebody says they don't like it here, that's an indicator they are going to leave. This is a helpful indicator, but it is much softer than just looking at the number of widgets you make. How someone feels about where they work will change – and it can change daily depending on the way the organization works. An employee engagement survey done after a stressful commute to the office or after a row at home will lead to a lower score. It is totally dependent on mood and completely subjective. The Likert scale will go some way to helping us turn it into data for the masses, but we have to be aware of the limitations of a survey and the need for conversation to help ensure what we believe is reality – you cannot rely on a survey alone to give you a robust picture of what is really going on.

Interpreting the data

More and more organizations are using data to make decisions. This is great, but making sure people have the skills to interpret that data accurately is another thing. It's easy to take the number of widgets made and declare 'this is great, we have made 53 widgets today' – but that doesn't tell you if this is good or bad in comparison to other days, and it also doesn't tell you about the quality of those widgets.

Much like when a communication audit tells you people prefer digital communication (not always the case) but doesn't tell you what content they want from that digital communication. We have to take the time to build the whole picture – the complete version of the reality based on what we need to understand to progress.

Making sure that the interpretation of the data is accurate must stem from clarity around the purpose for the data collection. The data that tells you there is a problem and things are in chaos is different from the data that will tell you why, and it will be different data that tells you if the fix is working.

We inherently group 'data' together. We want insights quickly so we often don't invest in the time or the right tools to enable us to forensically analyse what we find and we rush to get the 'is it working?' or 'does this show we are worthy?' results. Data is so much more than that and having the skills in the organization to understand the fundamentals of what people are thinking and experiencing is incredibly important if you want to get to the reality of a situation.

People diagnostics

There are lots of tests out there that explore individual personality and relationships. The most famous is the Myers–Briggs Type Indicator (MBTI), which is based on the work of Swiss psychiatrist Carl Jung. Jung was the first to discuss introverts and extroverts, and his work in this area was carried forward by mother and daughter Katharine Briggs and Isabel Briggs Myers. They worked to raise the awareness of Jung's personality types and were keen to share that there were no right or wrong jobs for individuals.

Their work was popular in the 1940s and by the 1980s it was the go-to personality test for organizations. It's so popular today that the four letters that 'describe you' can be found on online dating profiles to provide an indicator to another about who you are.

There are other tests though, and the two other popular ones are DISC and SDI.

What is important is that organizations choose the right one for them, and that the importance of context is applied. The tests don't cross over as while they are all focused on individuals, they look at them from different angles.

SDI stands for Strength Deployment Inventory. SDI helps people relate to one of seven Motivational Value Systems (MVS) and one of thirteen Conflict Sequences. It plays off people's basic need to better understand themselves and others, and that understanding allows them to lead with clarity and empathy, build stronger teams and more effectively navigate conflict. It's much more about the relationships with others than MBTI, which is focused on the individual.

DISC stands for Dominance, Influence, Steadiness and Conscientiousness. The model is based on the work of psychologist William Marston and it looks at people, pace and task. Again, this is different from the others and has a strong focus on the context for the behaviour.

When it comes to diagnosing what is happening inside an organization one of these people-diagnostic tools might be used. It usually depends on the preference of the organization as they are likely to be using one already, and if they are not, the choice of diagnostic comes down to the objective and the need.

If it is about the individual, MBTI. If it is about teams, SDI. And if it is about understanding task and pace in context, then DISC.

Whatever the objective, it is important to remember that these are indicators and not tests that suggest right or wrong.

Key points in this chapter

1 There is a lot to consider when it comes to diagnosing what is going on in the organization. There are different ways you can do this, from focus groups to listening interviews to surveys. Working with experts in data science will make sure that the bias is as removed as it can be from the data collection.

2 Find the right combination for your challenge. Know that if you have people feeling uncared for or ignored, a survey alone won't be enough. Explore the options to meet your needs and make sure you're asking the difficult questions.

3 The numbers of employees you're looking to gather data from will determine the method – I would always recommend listening interviews, as conversations provide a richer source of information and context.

4 Conducting listening interviews requires you to be present in the conversation and demonstrate active listening.

5 Focus groups can be a great way to find out how groups of people think and, if carried out after an online survey, they can verify findings. Keep them to a maximum of 10 people.

6 Using surveys and polls can be good ways to gather data quickly.

7 Benchmarking doesn't always tell you something. Make sure that if you are benchmarking your communication channels or any other communication aspect, you have a reason to and the comparison is needed.

8 Be mindful and aware of bias in collecting and interpreting data, and in the sample you use.

9 There are ways to explore people diagnostics – MBTI, DISC and SDI are all referenced here and are worth exploring if this is an area of interest or focus.

Quick tips

To help, here are some of the questions often used during this phase:

- What is the purpose of [team or company]?
- Do you know the strategy for the business? What the focus is for the next 12–24 months?
- What makes [team or company] different from other providers?
- What are the challenges about working at [company]?
- How do you find out about how the business is doing?

- What do you love about working here?
- Do you trust the leadership team?
- How do you find out about the industry you're in? What do you read/watch?
- Who are your main competitors?
- Do you feel safe at work?
- How often do you get together as a team?
- Do you feel valued?
- How long have you worked at [company] and in what capacity (contractor/employee)?
- What stops you from being able to do your job?
- What is the one thing we could do to make the communication inside the organization better?

References and further reading

Buolamwini, J (2018) Gender Shades, gendershades.org/ (archived at https://perma.cc/M4J3-QNWG)

Chalabi, M (2016) Weapons of Math Destruction: Cathy O'Neil adds up the damage of algorithms, *Guardian*, 27 October, www.theguardian.com/books/2016/oct/27/cathy-oneil-weapons-of-math-destruction-algorithms-big-data (archived at https://perma.cc/S5KF-QLM8)

Dastin, J (2018) Amazon scraps secret AI recruiting tool that showed bias against women, Reuters, 11 October, www.reuters.com/article/us-amazon-com-jobs-automation-insight/amazon-scraps-secret-ai-recruiting-tool-that-showed-bias-against-women-idUSKCN1MK08G (archived at https://perma.cc/YL9N-44JS)

Devlin, H (2018) Unconscious bias: What is it and can it be eliminated? *Guardian*, 2 December, www.theguardian.com/uk-news/2018/dec/02/unconscious-bias-what-is-it-and-can-it-be-eliminated (archived at https://perma.cc/4K4K-UUGX)

Elsesser, K (2019) Maybe the Apple and Goldman Sachs credit card isn't gender biased, *Forbes*, 14 November, www.forbes.com/sites/kimelsesser/

2019/11/14/maybe-the-apple-and-goldman-sachs-credit-card-isnt-gender-biased/#26ccc2641518 (archived at https://perma.cc/FL6Y-A5X8)

Gardner, D (2009) *The Science of Fear: How the culture of fear manipulates your brain*, Plume Books, New York

Jacoby, S M (1986) Employee attitude testing at Sears, Roebuck and Company, 1938–1960, *Business History Review*, **60** (4), pp 602–32

Knight, W (2019) The Apple Card didn't 'see' gender – and that's the problem, *Wired*, 19 November, www.wired.com/story/the-apple-card-didnt-see-genderand-thats-the-problem/ (archived at https://perma.cc/MU6M-42TX)

Knowledge@Wharton (2018) Personality puzzler: Is there any science behind the Myers–Briggs test?, knowledge.wharton.upenn.edu/article/does-the-myers-briggs-test-really-work/ (archived at https://perma.cc/G6DZ-JGV2)

Lapowski, I (2018) Google autocomplete still makes vile suggestions, *Wired*, 12 February, www.wired.com/story/google-autocomplete-vile-suggestions/ (archived at https://perma.cc/LL53-AC4M)

Lexico (nd) Data (Oxford dictionary definition), www.lexico.com/definition/data (archived at https://perma.cc/Q8K2-ZMDF)

Naidu, B (2016) SDI vs others, LinkedIn, 30 March, www.linkedin.com/pulse/sdi-vs-others-balaji-naidu/ (archived at https://perma.cc/86AL-ML6F)

Nasiripour, S and Natarajan, S (2019) Apple co-founder says Goldman's Apple Card algorithm discriminates, Bloomberg.com, 10 November, www.bloomberg.com/news/articles/2019-11-10/apple-co-founder-says-goldman-s-apple-card-algo-discriminates (archived at https://perma.cc/2WYW-H99L)

Nedland, E (2019) Apple Card is accused of gender bias. Here's how that can happen, CNN Business, 12 November, edition.cnn.com/2019/11/12/business/apple-card-gender-bias/index.html (archived at https://perma.cc/H4PP-7L9V)

Nuzzo, R (2014) Scientific method: Statistical errors: *P* values, the 'gold standard' of statistical validity, are not as reliable as many scientists assume, *Nature*, **506**

O'Neil, C (2017) The era of blind faith in big data must end, TED, www.ted.com/talks/cathy_o_neil_the_era_of_blind_faith_in_big_data_must_end?language=en (archived at https://perma.cc/4WJ3-TGFC)

O'Neil, C (2018) *Weapons of Math Destruction: How big data increases inequality and threatens democracy*, Penguin Books, London.

Singer, E (2012) The use and effects of incentives in surveys, iriss.stanford.edu/sites/g/files/sbiybj6196/f/singer_slides.pdf (archived at https://perma.cc/PQ62-9ZGY)

TotalSDI (2015) The power of the SDI, totalsdi.com/assessments/the-power-of-the-sdi/ (archived at https://perma.cc/9RN9-QXH2)

The fix 07

How to make changes that last

Once you have understood what's going on and diagnosed why it's happening, there are lots of ways to fix organizations or teams. While there are always different reasons things are happening, there are also usually core things that need to be fixed either at an organizational level or a team level. This is the final part of the Field Model and addresses the core areas to focus on for communications and organizations.

What's important is that you are fixing the bit that needs to be fixed, not the assumed issue or the symptom. You're taking action linked to facts and data that will allow you to measure and move forwards.

Just the other week a conversation went like this:

Client: I asked the operations managers to add on the task to their existing walk the floor and no one has done it yet.

Me: Why not?

Client: I don't know.

Me: Well, you need to ask them why they aren't doing it – but not in an accusatory way. Find out what's stopping them by asking questions like 'We talked about doing this last week, but I know it hasn't happened yet, is there anything you need from me to help?'

Client: They have said they don't have the time and also in some cases the right tools to do it.

Me: OK, so now we know more. The time thing is a myth as it is about priorities, but the right tools are important. You might have asked them to do something that is a bolt-on to an existing thing that doesn't work! Or that existing thing is something they hate doing. You need to delve into the issues underneath what's stopping them and then you can fix that.'

The next day the client emailed me to say they had woken up buzzing with ideas and ways to take things forward – and it had only been a 45-minute conversation.

We focused our time to discuss and drill into an issue. Being inquisitive about what is really going on is the only way to make sure the fix addresses the real problems inside the organization or the team.

How to fix

Fixing is done in a variety of ways. Quick things that can be done to help move things forward – this can often be making decisions. Decisions that haven't been made or have been ignored. In some cases, this is a decision the CEO or the MD needs to take, in others it is the whole leadership team together.

Fixing often involves a project, managed by an individual, to work through the things that need to change. There is usually a tactical list of activity, stuff that has been swept under the carpet. Alongside that is the hard stuff, the people stuff and the changing behaviours stuff.

So, imagine that I am coming into an organization you have worked in for 15 years to tell you that things need to change. To tell you that your behaviour is not OK. To tell you that we need to explore different ways of working in order to grow and achieve the strategy. You are not going to like me – and that is a totally normal reaction. We are nearly always defensive when someone is telling us we need to do something differently. There are difficult conversations in the fix and while some of these do need to be had by the CEO and HR, they need someone to organize them, rally people around and inject some pace into what needs to happen.

The fix fails if the leadership don't follow through, or the complexity of the organization is such that every element has to go further up the chain of command, taking time.

If the outcome of the fix is to reshape the organization following an M&A or to allow a founder to step back from the organization, things need to change and in some cases, no matter how much you treat people as individuals, they will be angry, they will be upset and they will not want to work through the process.

Sometimes things have to be pulled apart to be put back together. Ideally, things aren't so bad that this needs to happen but if no one has ever told you something isn't OK, why would you know it needs to change?

And that is the nub of the issue. It's easy to relate some of this to parenting – if you constantly pick up the toys why would the child learn to tidy up? If you cover up for people, allow things to happen even though you don't agree with them, you're contributing to a toxic workplace. And a workplace should never be toxic. It should be a place where people enjoy spending their time. They should be encouraged to thrive, develop and grow. To work together and to understand how they contribute to success.

Don't underestimate this. Changing an organization or a team is hard. Being an outsider is easy because you can make change happen with less emotional attachment and you can work at pace because you're only focused on delivering the fixes. The challenge is helping people accept that they have to change too.

We have established that the fix has to include an aspect of people, which in turn links to relationships. But we also have to look at procedures or processes as these are often a contributing factor to the chaos.

There is some theory that backs up this approach and that's the 'Hamburger Model' developed by Cockman *et al*, which shows a straight horizontal arrow to represent the task, with a curved arrow from start to finish over the top for processes and the same underneath for relationships.

What this shows is the importance of all factors when it comes to completing the task at hand. The task can be big or small (company goal/ team objective) but to complete it successfully, you need all three aspects working together.

- The task is the content of the work. We have touched on the need to explore what the organization does, how a widget goes from A to B for example – that's the task.

- The procedure is the how – who does what, by when, what happens next – it's the step by step. Often for organizations this is an ISO process that has been developed as well.

- And then there are relationships – the inclusion, the power, the conflict, the decision makers, the emotion.

When you consider all three of these factors within your organization, you are sure to gain some idea as to where the chaos is and where the fix needs to come from.

It's also why the fix will usually include a RASCI to help everyone understand where decision-making lies. Some may be more familiar with RACI but adding in the S allows for the role of support, which can be very useful:

Responsible: The doer.
Accountable: The buck stops here.
Support: The helper.
Consult: In the loop.
Inform: Notify me.

These can be overused but they can also be a great way to start to align everyone to the process to achieve the task. Make a list of tasks in a column on the left and a column for each RASCI. Only one name can go in the Responsible and Accountable boxes, multiple names can go in the others.

I mentioned that the set of fixes for every team or organization is different. There are always bespoke aspects to the issues and there are always bespoke fixes but the themes that come up almost every time are:

- Leadership: There will usually be a need to address leadership skills – from line managers through to more senior people in the organization.

- Blockers: There are often individuals who will block any transformation inside an organization – being able to identify them is important.

- Culture: 'The way things work around here'. Is the company culture what people think it is, is it being done for the sake of it, to tick a box? What should it really be?

- Strategy: A lack of understanding in terms of the direction, why things are happening and where decisions are made.

Overarching all of these is purpose.

Purpose

Purpose is something that comes up a lot when we start to explore people and organizations. It's the overarching theme because it works on an individual level as well as an organizational one.

As individuals, we are more motivated and more satisfied with purpose. As an organization, we are more successful being purpose-led.

In 2019, Kantar conducted a study into the role of purpose in organizations (Kantar, 2020). The study outlined three phases for organizations to work through to become purpose-led: articulation, infusion and amplification. The study suggests that working through these stages takes an organization from using purpose as an isolated tactic to becoming a purpose-led movement.

We know that purpose is needed inside organizations to help employees engage in something bigger than profit. To help them feel they are part of something. When it comes to fix, it's important to have a little delve into why it could be causing chaos.

Purpose and strategy go hand in hand. If people don't know why they are doing something, it will be harder for them to actually do anything. We need a sense of purpose to be motivated, so we need to know how it links to something overall.

This can be hard for organizations where the focus is on profit. It can be argued that having a focus on profit still provides a strong strategic narrative and we know from the work of Macleod and Clarke covered earlier (Chapter 1) that this is one of the four enablers of engagement. More and more research is coming out about the role of purpose and its importance.

Simon Farrell provided some insight into the area of purpose. As a brand expert and co-founder of Today the Arena, he has devoted his career to exploring the role of brand, purpose and culture. His equation of what gives a business purpose links together leadership,

Table 7.1   Simon Farrell's equation of purpose

PB = C⁴ × SS × ES × EP™				
Purposeful business	Conscious Clarity Connected Committed	Soulful solutions	Ethical standards	Enough profit

products and ethics to reinforce the fact this cannot be a tick-box exercise (Table 7.1).

Aware that not everyone wants to be purpose-led, Farrell suggests there is a place for organizations to be purposeful. This is important because not everyone wants to start a movement and change the world, but everyone can contribute.

When it comes to your organization and looking at purpose, I'd recommend you consider these things:

- Why do you exist as an organization?
- What are you doing to achieve that? This should be a big list of activity that is happening and possibly stuff that isn't, but that you'd like to do.
- Who else is doing this? This will help you explore purposeful vs purpose-led.
- Does everyone in the leadership team know this and agree with it? Explore their individual purpose at the same time, as this could unlock other things to help both the personal and the organization's cause.

Business unusual

Perhaps one of the best examples of a purpose-led company is clothing brand, Patagonia. Founded by climbers and surfers, its wholesome values centre around a minimalist way of life, enjoying the great outdoors and acting on pressing environmental issues.

What sets Patagonia apart today is that it leads with its story, rather than its products. This connects with mounting consumer social consciousness; 62 per cent of consumers want companies to stand up for issues they're passionate about. Through its strapline, 'We're in business to save our home planet', Patagonia is clearly part of a movement for change. How many clothing websites have 'activism' as a menu option?

True purpose-led companies have a strong aspiration at their core from the outset; it's something that's difficult to reverse engineer. Patagonia started in the late 1950s when avid climber Yvon Chouinard began selling pitons for rock climbing from the back of his car. The business grew, but when he saw the tools were damaging the fragile rock, he created an aluminium chock that could be wedged in by hand, rather than hammered.

As the range expanded to encompass colourful clothing for exploring wild places, Patagonia also became known as a company that protects those environments. Its grassroots activism was prompted in the 1970s by an environmental issue close to its headquarters. Officials threatened to divert the Ventura river, claiming the river was dead. The outlook was grim until a group, spearheaded by Patagonia, joined the city council meeting and disproved claims; showing photos of the birds, muskrats and water snakes that spawned on the estuary. The river was restored.

It didn't stop there. Patagonia has a self-imposed Earth tax; 1 per cent of profits are ploughed into environmental non-profits working to protect air, land and water. Employees use 'their roles in the sports community to drive positive social and environmental change'. Patagonia Action Works enables people to 'discover events, petitions and skilled volunteering opportunities' as well as 'donate money to local causes'. It created a whole new organic cotton supply chain and also joined forces with Columbia Sportswear in a lawsuit challenging President Trump's attempts to roll back Obama's Clean Power Plan.

This purpose, along with a focus on the long-term, means Patagonia maintains profitability. Corley Kenna, Director of Global Communications explains, 'We all feel equally part of the mission, regardless of one's level or role, and it's always our North Star for business strategy… We always take the long view… We've found that when we put the planet first and do the right things for the planet, it winds up being good for business. It has proven itself over and over again.'

The company has become a true movement. It spends more time advocating environmental causes than on marketing products. Not every company can be purpose-led, but as brands that claim to be are being tested more than ever, companies like Patagonia are setting the standard.

Feet on the ground – how to create a purposeful company

Founded in 2007, TOMS has been purposeful from the outset. 'It was a simple concept: sell a pair of shoes today, give a pair of shoes tomorrow', explains Blake Mycoskie, founder of TOMS, or Tomorrow's Shoes. While travelling in Argentina, Blake saw the suffering of children growing up without shoes. More than 1.5 billion people have a soil-transmitted infection and shoes help protect against this, as well as against injury. After selling his first 10,000 shoes, Blake gave 10,000 shoes to children in need in Argentina.

While some companies can be purpose-led, it's also possible operate in a way that's purposeful – playing a part by contributing. Brands that offer more than meeting consumer needs make an increasingly lasting impact on consumers.

TOMS has expanded beyond lightweight shoes to include a vegan shoe collection, sunglasses and coffee. Its mission to improve lives through business has meant that over 95 million pairs of shoes have been donated, including canvas slip-ons, wet weather slip-ons, school shoes and athletic shoes.

TOMS has since expanded on the one-for-one model and now dedicates at least one-third of profits to a fund managed by its Giving Team. In 2011, TOMS Eyewear was launched and has provided medical treatment, and funded prescription glasses and over 780,000 sight restorations. Similarly, TOMS Roasting Co helps provide safe living conditions to developing communities through sustainable water systems; so far funding 722,000 weeks of safe water. It has given $6.5 million in impact grants across 85 countries. Unsurprisingly, Blake's book, *Start Something That Matters* was a *New York Times* bestseller.

But it's not a perfect story; as with any success, there are bumps in the road. In 2012, Blake took a sabbatical; his 'reason for being now felt like a job'. It was during this time that he read Simon Sinek's *Start with Why* and realized he'd become more focused on the process than the purpose, 'We'd forgotten our overarching mission, which is to use business to improve lives. That is our greatest competitive advantage: It allows us to build an emotional bond with customers and motivate employees, because they know they are shopping and working for a movement bigger than themselves.'

He returned to make TOMS a movement again and now promotes gun safety following the mass shootings in Thousand Oaks, California. In an emotional appearance on *The Tonight Show with Jimmy Fallon,* he announced a $5 million donation to end gun violence. With this move, TOMS used its website as a hub for action to call for universal background checks.

As Blake says in his book, 'Conscious capitalism is about more than simply making money – although it's about that too. It's about creating a successful business that also connects supporters to something that matters to them and that has great impact in the world.'

Having a clear purpose flows through into the culture and communication inside the organization. It provides employees with a core to the activity they are doing that isn't about profit and in turn, it signals a greater need for the work to be done.

As you look at the fix for the organization and how to move forward, articulating your purpose will be key. For the internal communicator, it ensures the messaging and content is aligned to something everyone can get behind as well.

Leadership behaviours

Being purposeful or purpose-led requires a strong sense of leadership. But when it comes to the fix, the leadership behaviours always come up as something to explore.

It could be an individual or it can be a whole team – either way, it will be on the list.

Integrity

Leadership behaviour is a tough one. Firstly, no one is expecting anyone to be perfect – we are human. But the one thing people do expect is integrity. And quite often, the biggest issue employees have is that things are said, but nothing is done. That say–do gap is integrity.

Saying to a leader that their issue is integrity is a tough one. It's an incredibly emotive word and it's something many of us value highly in others, but where we have a blind spot in ourselves.

As a team or a group of leaders, discussing strengths and weaknesses is important. Discussing challenges and how to overcome them is equally important. Being able to trust each other is a must. If trust and fear are important to us as human beings, we must remember that the leadership title doesn't counter the human being. We don't stop having all the same subconscious, innate thoughts that we need to survive.

So, what are the behaviours that come up and how do we fix them? Behaviours that should be explored to enable the fix:

- Lack of decision making.
- Being too busy for people.
- Saying one thing and doing another.
- Not following through on an action that is linked to someone's career/development.
- Being inconsistent with communication.
- Not working as a team, looking after own interests.
- Sharing unverified information or data that isn't accurate.

A lot of this links to empathy. It links to a need to explore vulnerability and courage, and the ability to be genuine in the workplace.

We talked about different leadership approaches earlier in the book. When it comes to exploring how they need to change for the benefit of the organization and the success of teams, it's important to explore the right style for you. While I would advocate for servant leadership with a focus on empathy, for many this isn't natural – and if we were all the same it would be a very strange world.

It has to be genuine. You cannot lead a team or empower those around you if you don't believe in what you are doing. A good leader is one that is honest and genuine – so it's about finding the ways to unlock those aspects of the individual to remove the chaos.

This is where the role of coaching comes in. Those who receive some form of coaching report increases in self-confidence and benefit from improved performance. In addition, they comment on improved relationships, and better communication skills as a result.

The benefits of coaching are proven, and working with someone to discuss your communication style and impact is so important in leadership. A CEO once said to me, 'I sometimes forget that my words and actions carry more weight than others.'

They say with great power comes great responsibility – but underneath the power and the responsibility is still a human being who is emotionally led.

Working as a team

Working with individuals is one part of the fix but there is often a need to explore the whole team. This is where things like SDI (Strength Deployment Inventory) come back into play and it also demonstrates the non-linear aspect of this model. The Field Model has diagnosed that leadership is an issue. But further diagnosis is needed to delve into what's happening across the team and for the individual.

Patrick Lencioni talks about five dysfunctions of a team. This is a good summary of the challenges, specifically in a leadership environment:

- Absence of trust: The fear of being vulnerable with team members prevents the building of trust within teams.
- Fear of conflict: The desire to preserve artificial harmony stifles the occurrence of productive ideological conflict.
- Lack of commitment: The lack of clarity or buy-in prevents team members from making decisions they will stick to.
- Avoidance of accountability: The need to avoid interpersonal discomfort prevents team members from holding one another accountable.
- Inattention to results: The pursuit of individual goals and personal status erodes the focus on collective success.

As a team, working together is important. As a leadership team, if you are not working together that fractured state will transfer through the organization. It comes up a lot with operations, sales teams and support functions. The fix is always communication. Discussing as a team what's going on, why there isn't the openness and honesty and what that really means.

You'll know it's a team issue, rather than an individual issue when:

- You hear the same issues from different parts of the team, suggesting fractured relationships.
- Individuals are focused on themselves and their own goals, not working for the good of the team.
- A lack of understanding from everyone about others and the focus of those individuals or teams.
- Lack of a common goal.

Interestingly, trust is not usually an indicator of an issue. People will often trust those around them easily. There is a need to discuss to what degree that trust stretches and what it feels like to them. If you just ask people if they trust someone, it won't tell you much about what impact that has on the relationship or their ability to work together.

Line managers

Line manager behaviours are hugely important. A lot can be focused on those at the top, the relationship between those on the board, but little attention is paid to line managers who actually have more power when it comes to some of the usual key performance indicators (KPIs) organizations look at.

People leave managers, they don't leave organizations. Perhaps because emotions often lead the way, but also because relationships matter. The little attention that is paid to line managers, for those in internal communication, is usually a cause of the barrier to successful information flow. But the lack of investment in skills to help them manage relationships, communicate effectively and have difficult conversations is a fundamental part of the chaos that is happening.

There are tons of development programmes available for line managers but there is a significant lack of organizations investing in this and making time for it. It's time to address this imbalance and invest in the relationships across the organization.

The Richer Way: How great leadership starts with treating people well

Some leaders have a natural ability to inspire people. They have a different way of thinking about business, employees and consumers that makes a huge difference. Julian Richer, founder of Richer Sounds, is one of those people. Starting the business in 1978, aged 19, he opened his first shop on London Bridge Walk. The company is now the UK's biggest hi-fi and home cinema retailer, with annual sales of nearly £200 million. It owns the buildings for most of its 52 stores and holds the record for the highest sales per square foot of any retailer in the world. After years of success, and with retirement in mind, in 2019 Richer converted the business to an employee owned trust.

Richer was inspired early on by *In Search of Excellence*, published in 1982, by Tom Peters and Robert Waterman. The book cites respect and development for employees and being customer-centric as key factors of excellence. Richer went on to write *The Richer Way*, to explain how he had put this knowledge into practice. The essence of his leadership style is very simple; as Richer says, 'Most people you meet are decent and, if you treat them well, they'll treat you well back.'

Treating people well doesn't need to involve complex programmes. It's the seemingly small things like Richer's regular emails of thanks to shops with good figures; something that's easy for leaders to overlook. Recognizing employee loyalty and good sales, and providing secure, well-paid jobs has resulted in an annual staff turnover of less than half the average of UK retailers.

Putting customers and staff at the heart of the business means Richer is called on to advise other leading businesses, including M&S, where he focused on engagement, motivation and driving cultural change through staff communication.

When we talk about integrity and closing the 'say–do' gap, it's clear to see why Richer's leadership is universally praised. He believes happy colleagues equal happy customers. As well as giving away 60 per cent of his shares and dividing out £3.5 million among his employees in 2019, Richer Sounds also provides company-paid holiday homes, private medical support, subsidized gym membership and a Helping Hand fund in case of emergencies.

'Experience Better is at the heart of the Richer Sounds' philosophy', as Richer explains in *The Ethical Capitalist*. 'I mean treating staff, customers and suppliers honestly, openly and respectfully. I mean doing what we say we will do. I mean taking responsibility for our actions, owning up when things go wrong and setting out to put them right. I mean seeing ourselves as an integral part of society and paying our dues – especially taxes – accordingly.'

Richer remains a campaigner for better corporate leadership. He says, 'By following this approach, I believe we create a virtuous circle for ourselves: Not only is it the right thing to do, we sleep better at night, and I believe a fair and honest approach to customers and staff leads to a huge competitive advantage.'

Leaders can learn from Richer by developing skills such as great decision making and personal resilience. Implementing policies such as making yourself available for your people, doing what you say you'll do, communicating consistently and listening carefully prove that all this can be done while keeping your business profitable.

Blockers or toxic people

This is one of the hardest conversations to have. Sometimes there are people who need to leave an organization, and usually this is because it would be better both for the organization and for them. They can be identified by their lack of engagement in the organization, resentment of the management, impact on others (others mention them as hard to work with), lack of self-awareness or desire to change – the list can go on.

What's important to notice are any trends that may develop in conversations with various employees, and not just an individual grudge – that isn't the same. When the patterns emerge, you can see whether the individual needs to leave or just move into a different role – sometimes that is the issue alone.

When an employee lacks the desire to change, or awareness and care of their impact on others, then it's time for them to move on. Organizations change over time and sometimes, big changes like mergers or acquisitions mean it isn't the same place it was years ago. This is OK, but we all need to recognize when we aren't happy in a role and it's time to move on.

The impact of blockers/toxic people is huge. Behaviour breeds behaviour and that is the same whether it's positive or negative. Those people who hate the work, hate the company and love being in misery will bring everyone down with them. If they refuse to follow processes, the impact on others is huge. No one person is an island when it comes to working inside an organization. No matter where you 'sit' in the organization, working with others will be needed.

Blocking other people from being able to do their job is not going to help the team or the organization achieve its goals.

When it comes to the fix, it's about having the difficult conversation with the individual in line with the broader organizational strategy. The conversations you'll need to have will be around organizational design and the skills of the team in the structure of the function.

Internal communication is not an island. When it comes to looking at how an organization operates, organizational design has to play a role. Right person, right role – often a phrase used in HR. Investing in the skills inside the organization to look at the design or the teams and structures is really important because without a focus on people there will be chaos.

Culture

In 2013 a *Harvard Business Review* article cited different definitions for organizational culture:

- Culture is how organizations do things.
- Organizational culture is the sum of values and rituals which serve as 'glue' to integrate the members of the organization.
- Culture is the organization's immune system.
- Organizational culture [is shaped by] the main culture of the society we live in, albeit with greater emphasis on particular parts of it.

When we define culture, we talk about how things happen around here. It's the way people interact, the language that is used – it's all the things that play out in national cultures or your culture at home – just in the workplace.

We get very hung up on organizational culture. A lot of it links to purpose, but culture is highlighted in the fix part of the model consistently because it is often a tick-box exercise. This means that no one has given much thought to what the culture is, partly because no one is linking behaviours and values back to the purpose of the organization. As a result, things like 'culture clubs' are created, so it becomes the responsibility of a few people. There is apathy towards these activities; comments like 'Why do I have to be the one to arrange it all?' are often heard.

Culture shouldn't be forced. That said, there are times when you need to nudge the culture in a different direction. Things can get stale, teams can get stuck in how things happen and if there has been a combination of poor leadership and toxic people, the culture will need a very specific focus.

The nudge aspect is important – culture doesn't change overnight, no matter what happens. It will take time but when it comes to exploring the chaos, the culture has to play a role. What is acceptable? What is allowed? What is not OK? These are all questions that need to be asked as you explore how things get done.

As organizations change to respond to factors outside of their walls, the culture has to adapt. Not many people were prepared for the global pandemic in 2020 that forced almost the whole world to work from their homes.

The impact on culture could not be ignored – but for many, it was an easy trap to fall into. It showed that culture is not about the walls of an office. It's about how you communicate with each other, how you work together during challenging times and how you support each other. At a time where communication became so important for organizational success, culture was a focus for many organizations.

As the world of work changed, the need to look at the ways of working was paramount. It's about the purpose of the organization, what's important and how people feel about being at work.

Culture as the organization's immune system is an important definition from the list in the *HBR* article. For some, it is the culture and the values that underpin it that ensure survival in a crisis. There are those in the Metropolitan Police who credit their ability to work through crisis effectively to the alignment to values. As values shape beliefs and attitudes, making them part of your response is important.

If we were to look at the fix as an equation, we could suggest that the purpose comes from adding culture and strategy together. Within culture there are the values, beliefs and behaviours. The plan and activities create the strategy. Combined, this creates the purpose, or the why. It's the emotional part of the organization. The alignment of all of these together completes the puzzle of an organization.

Strategy

The strategy is always part of the fix. This is because diagnosis will often report that employees don't know it, it isn't clear or they don't know how their role is linked to it.

And for some at the top, this is baffling. 'We talk about it all the time' they will say. Indeed, YOU do. But do you talk about it in the context of the different roles or tasks across the organization? Have employees been involved in shaping the content of the strategy against the framework set by the board?

A strategy always exists. Even if it is created from the ground up – it will be there. Articulating it in a way that inspires others and focuses the tasks across the organization is the part around strategy that is often forgotten. The strategy is often linked to investors or analysts and their need to know what is going on for shareholders – but employees are fundamental stakeholders here and shouldn't be ignored.

You cannot deliver a strategy without people. The whole organization has to come together, work together, to deliver the strategy. To work together effectively, relationships and trust are needed, and these come from effective communication.

For communication to be effective and influential it has to be consistent and ongoing. You cannot launch a strategy and never speak of it again. At the same time, you have to make sure that the strategy is a story to be told. A story relevant to those in any role inside the organization.

A strategy as a framework, with central activity, makes communicating it an easy task. Teams can take ownership of the framework by populating the activity with things that are relevant to them.

SSP – strategic framework helps make customers smile

Food travel company SSP creates and runs food outlets in locations where people are on the move. With a portfolio of over 550 brands, including Burger King, Jamie Oliver, Ritazza and YO! Sushi, SSP has 39,000 employees and a presence in 35 countries.

Communicating and implementing a strategy consistently across a huge and diverse workforce like SSP's is crucial. Often a strategy is communicated by senior leadership and then left to interpretation; SSP realized success would depend on its people playing an equal role in strategy delivery.

SSP's vision is to be the number one food and beverage brand in travel locations worldwide. In the UK, this was articulated through a mission to 'put a SMILE on every customer's face'. The company developed a strategic framework to make every element of the strategy relevant to every employee.

Using the acronym SMILE, each initial represented a core pillar of the strategy:

Sustainable profitable growth
Memorable experience
Inspire each other
Love food
Expert innovators

With a framework, activities at a senior operational level like new training initiatives or product development can support this. Managers make the strategy relevant in stores, giving a sense of ownership to create memorable experiences through food tastings or monthly competitions. Creating a thread that runs throughout the organization and linking daily activities to each pillar makes it cyclical, as opposed to top down. The simplicity of SMILE made it an easy strategy to launch at SSP's annual conference, where it achieved 86 per cent strategic engagement.

When the business floated in 2014, it needed a strategy that worked globally. A strategic framework was developed using 'five levers of growth', with each lever having five subset elements to drive progress. The five levers can be applied universally, whether a Starbucks in New York or an Upper Crust at Waterloo station, with activities tailored by country depending on its maturity. The strategic framework achieved buy-in across the company since every employee could make it personally relevant every day.

Whether your strategy revolves around revenue growth, mergers and acquisitions, productivity or culture, a framework allows you to tweak the language and the focus for individuals and teams. Every part of the business can directly respond to the strategy because linking the subsets to actionable activities keeps goals in focus.

Key points in this chapter

1 In the fix phase you are fixing the things that need your attention and not busy doing things that won't have an impact. You're not working from assumption. You're taking action linked to facts and data that will allow you to measure and move forward.

2 Asking questions to understand why things are happening should take place now and it should be allowing you to focus on fixing specifics.

3 Exploring how the task, process and relationships link together is important. You have to explore relationships in order to impact the task and this in turn plays out in the processes. Ignoring the relationships around a task will make it harder to complete, even with amazing processes in place.

4 Look at the RASCI model to enable decision making and accountability; Responsible, Accountable, Support, Consult, Inform.

5 Having a clear purpose is so important for an organization. Explore whether your organization is purposeful and/or purpose-led – examples from Patagonia and TOMS show how purpose can play out inside organizations.

6 The fix fails if the leadership don't follow through, or the complexity of the organization is such that every element has to go further up the chain of command, taking time.

7 Leadership behaviours around integrity, teamwork and the role of line managers are important areas to focus on.

8 Blockers, culture, leadership and strategy are the four core components to fix inside organizations. Focusing on them with a communication viewpoint means you are looking at them with a view to changing relationships and how things connect internally.

9 Culture can have many definitions – consider it as the way things get done inside your organization. Culture and communication are intrinsically linked.

10 Organizational strategy links to purpose and should always be in the fix – mainly because it is linked to the need for a corporate narrative, which we know is linked to driving employee engagement.

11 Leadership challenges are common and identifying them as a team is important to move forward. Coaching as a support tool is incredibly powerful for those in leadership roles.

12 A strategy can be created from the top or the ground up, or both. Exploring a strategy from both sides will enable one to be created that reflects everyone in the organization.

Quick tips

- Don't worry if there is no strategy from the leadership team – you can create one from the ground up.

- Invest in yourself to manage the fix. There are difficult conversations to have so make sure you have read the chapters here around people and you've explored the skills needed for managing conflict and change.

- Be consistent in your approach and demonstrate the behaviours of leadership outlined in this chapter to create and build trust.

References and further reading

Accenture (2018) To affinity and beyond: From me to we, the rise of the purpose-led brand, www.accenture.com/_acnmedia/thought-leadership-assets/pdf/accenture-competitiveagility-gcpr-pov.pdf (archived at https://perma.cc/C6G6-UFM4)

Anzilotti, E (2018) Why TOMS is taking a stand to end gun violence, Fast Company, 20 November, www.fastcompany.com/90270094/why-toms-is-taking-a-stand-to-end-gun-violence (archived at https://perma.cc/P4EH-83M3)

Association of Facilitators (2015), Foundations in Facilitation Skills Programme, www.associationoffacilitators.co.uk/ (archived at https://perma.cc/2WMG-HA57)

Fallon, J (2018) Toms founder Blake Mycoskie announces $5 million donation to end gun violence, YouTube, www.youtube.com/watch?v=s6msveTjZXQ (archived at https://perma.cc/GJ39-XNNN)

Farrell, S (nd) The algebra of purpose, Today the Arena, www.todaythearena.com/new-blog/2020/2/7/the-algebra-of-purpose (archived at https://perma.cc/LZH6-ENC4)

Institute of Coaching (2015) Benefits of coaching, instituteofcoaching.org/coaching-overview/coaching-benefits#:~:text=The%20benefits%20of%20coaching%20are (archived at https://perma.cc/JJD6-ZFK4)

Kantar Consulting (2020) Purpose 2020: Inspiring purpose-led growth, kantar.no/globalassets/ekspertiseomrader/merkevarebygging/purpose-2020/p2020-frokostseminar-250418.pdf (archived at https://perma.cc/8HZZ-67ED)

Lencioni, P (2012) *The Five Dysfunctions of a Team: Facilitator's Guide: The official guide to conducting the five dysfunctions workshops for teams and team leaders*, Pfeiffer, San Francisco, CA

Mainwaring, S (2018) Purpose at work: Lessons from TOMS on how to lead with purpose, *Forbes*, 13 December, www.forbes.com/sites/simonmainwaring/2018/12/13/purpose-at-work-lessons-from-toms-on-how-to-lead-with-purpose/#53921183e81b (archived at https://perma.cc/HX8Y-8DNJ)

Mau, D (2019) Toms shifts away from one for one, the giving model it originated, *Fashionista*, 20 November, fashionista.com/2019/11/toms-evolves-one-for-one-model (archived at https://perma.cc/9ZKR-KPZ8)

Mehta, B (2013) Engagement, what's missing? *Training Journal*, April

Moules, J (2019) Julian Richer: Treating people well pays dividends, ft.com, 20 October, www.ft.com/content/3ff0250a-e8ea-11e9-85f4-d00e5018f061 (archived at https://perma.cc/4Y79-RWR9)

Mycoskie, B (2012) *Start Something That Matters*, Virgin Books, New York

Mycoskie, B (2016) The founder of TOMS on reimagining the company's mission, *Harvard Business Review*, hbr.org/2016/01/the-founder-of-toms-on-reimagining-the-companys-mission (archived at https://perma.cc/2GB5-UKA3)

Patagonia (nd) Activism, www.patagonia.com/activism/ (archived at https://perma.cc/GN65-8PGP)

Richer, J (1995) *The Richer Way*, Penguin Random House, London

Richer, J (2019) *The Ethical Capitalist: How to make business work better for society*, Random House, London

Richer Sounds (2019) The Richer way: Our culture explained, www.richersounds.com/information/the_richer_way (archived at https://perma.cc/U69G-4PKE)

Shmukler, C (2020) Iconic outdoor brands Patagonia and Columbia support lawsuit to block Trump's environmental rollbacks, *Hatch*, 8 May, www.hatchmag.com/articles/iconic-outdoor-brands-patagonia-and-columbia-support-lawsuit/7715043 (archived at https://perma.cc/PSS5-8VFL)

Sonsev, V (2019) Patagonia's focus on its brand purpose is great for business, *Forbes*, 27 November, www.forbes.com/sites/veronikasonsev/2019/11/27/patagonias-focus-on-its-brand-purpose-is-great-for-business/#203d7ca54cb8 (archived at https://perma.cc/PTG9-K9Y9)

TOMS Shoes (2014) TOMS Shoes, http://tomsteamtwo.weebly.com/ (archived at https://perma.cc/PA82-P2BM)

Waller-Davies, B (2018) M&S hires Julian Richer to drive cultural change, *Retail Week*, 21 March, www.retail-week.com/people/mands-hires-julian-richer-to-drive-cultural-change-/7028701.article?authent=1 (archived at https://perma.cc/K3WV-Z8NP)

Wood, Z (2019) Richer Sounds founder hands over control of hi-fi and TV firm to staff, *Guardian*, 14 May, www.theguardian.com/business/2019/may/14/richer-sounds-staff-julian-richer (archived at https://perma.cc/4DJ4-EZ27)

Applying the model and making it work for the long term

08

Making the model work for the long term so that your internal communication is effective and influential requires every component to come together. The size of the organization or the team will determine how long things take to shift and the time investment required. The openness of individuals and the acceptance of individual change will also play an important role. This is often a journey of learning about the organization but also learning about yourself, and we all work at different speeds.

The skills we have learnt throughout the book to better understand people and organizations have to be applied here. As we apply the model in practical terms, we have to recognize that there is a need to take everyone on the journey and this in itself takes time. What shouldn't be underestimated is the time required for conversations around this change. Explaining the story around the process, what it means for the organization and spending time taking people through the plan is as important as the model itself.

In this chapter we will explore the application of the model to teams, to mergers and acquisitions, to growth and more. We will talk about the application of each phase in these areas so that you can explore the method with a map to follow. There are suggested time frames throughout but for every organization this will be different.

For some organizations there will be a familiarity with change and the journey that comes with it but for others this will feel very alien. In many cases conversations are happening that have never happened before and allowing time for that alone is important.

To help you work through the model there are a series of tables throughout this chapter that outline the chaos, the suggested diagnostic tool and the themes to look out for. There is also a suggested fix that will help you look at what's needed to move forwards. The timescales are estimates, but again provide you with an indication of investment for the change from chaos to calm.

Each table includes a range of timescales for the fixes. This is in part down to the individuals involved. Some people will respond well and adapt, and others will look to move on or continue in the same way. Most of the time you're working with changing behaviours and that's why the timescales are broad.

Fixing teams

When the issue is about teams, it's usually going to bubble up to be broader and impact the wider organization, but let's start here. The model can be applied no matter what the size of the organization, so working with teams on their level is a great basis. The model has already been applied to organizations with hundreds of employees and teams of fewer than ten.

Going through the steps of the model, we have to start by understanding what's wrong with the team. Where is the chaos? Here are some examples of chaos specifically linked to teams:

- People aren't getting along.
- Team A and Team B don't work well together, and we need them to.
- The team do their work in shifts and information is missed.
- Individual A thinks they are more important than individual B, and it's causing friction.

Now we have an understanding around what is going on.

When looking at teams one of the first things to discuss is whether or not it is actually a team. Sometimes people work in a function because it is easy from a hierarchy perspective. But they are not a team based on complementary skills.

In 2019 research into deskless workers (Redefining Communications, 2019) highlighted the importance of understanding teams when it comes to work. The research identified three types of groups within organizations: team, mixed and solitary. In the Remotely Interested research report the definitions are:

- Solitary: These are workers who don't need anyone else to do their job. Their work is carried out on their own and they only see people they work with during breaks or at the start/end of their working day. An example would be a bus driver.
- Mixed: The individual might work in a team at times and on their own in others. It means that their interactions with others are a mix of work and social. This would be those working in hospitality.
- Team: Working in a team and being reliant on each other to complete a task is very different to other ways of working. A true team brings different skills together to complement each other and overcome a challenge. A team of firefighters would be an example.

While this focused on the deskless workforce, the same can be said for 'teams' that exist in a support function or office capacity. Sometimes departments are made up of individual functions that naturally sit in one place to report to a senior member of staff. This does not make them a team.

So when a team isn't working well, you have to establish if it is, in fact, a team at all. Why do they need to work well together? What does it help? What does it hinder when they don't? What are the reasons we need them to work better together?

Similar questions are often asked when organizations need help creating a collaborative culture. We have to ask why that culture is needed, which bits of the organization need to collaborate and why.

All of these questions need to be asked throughout the diagnosis phase. The reasons why it might not be working so well could be because they are being forced into a team environment when they don't need to be.

The diagnosis will include talking to individuals to understand more about their role and how they connect with others. Why they connect with them (what's the reason for conversation/meetings, etc?), and it will also need to look at the business process. Do these teams need to connect, are there better ways of doing this, what does each team need to be successful?

It's also about understanding the individuals in the team and their combined goals. Their leadership might have them set on a path that is juxtaposed to the other teams. There could be anything going on but there is always a reason for behaviour. There is always a story we will tell ourselves about why that behaviour is happening.

The story is usually fiction so taking the time to work with facts and data instead of assumptions means we can make long-term changes.

So – we have understood what's going on in the team. As we diagnose what's going on we conduct listening interviews with a sample of people in the team. We can then explore the themes and begin to fix them. There will be uncomfortable conversations. There will be a need to explore self-development and self-awareness.

But we know from Chapter 4 on understanding people that we cannot fix things without stepping into vulnerability and bravery, and we know that there has to be some element of self-reflection in order to move forwards.

Being part of a team can be difficult. There are sometimes person-alities that clash, people we don't like very much – but that shouldn't stop teamwork. A team is not about being friends. It's about being respectful of each other and trusting each other – that is not the same as friendship. In addition, it is not about everyone being the same. A team should combine skills that complement each other and balance strengths and weaknesses – a factor that is often forgotten as we are wired to work with people like us.

Table 8.1 outlines the phases of the model applied to fixing teams, based on the symptoms outlined at the start of this section in this chapter.

Table 8.1 Fixing teams using the Field Model

Understand the chaos	Diagnostic tool	Diagnostic themes to explore	The fix	Timescale – team size dependent
People aren't getting along in the same team and it's causing issues for everyone	Listening interviews with individuals and peers	Relationships across the team generally Relationship of the team to the leader Understanding of team purpose Individual purpose	SDI could be recommended to better understand strengths and anchors Coaching conversations with individuals and teams	1–6 months
Team A and Team B don't work well together, and we need them to	Listening interviews (plus a survey, depending on size of team)	Why the teams need to work together What's the benefit of them working well together Role of the leaders in each team and their relationship	Process for the task to be completed to be reviewed Leader relationship coached through to working better together	3–9 months
The team work in shifts and things are missed	1:1 leadership interviews and survey	Get underneath the process or what is stopping the communication flow Leadership to explore their impact on others	Communication channels/training for managers Task review per shift and shift patterns	1–6 months
Individual A thinks they are more important than individual B and it's causing friction	1:1 interviews with each individual – same question set for both	Vulnerability and fear Self-development Personal goals	Coaching	1–9 months

Fixing a merger or acquisition

This is a longer journey than that for teams. And when it comes to the longer-term view, there are a lot of things to consider here.

When companies merge there is a need to explore what the new company feels and looks like. Does it have a whole new name, what is the organizational structure to support it, how do the teams work together, how do you launch to market – there is a long list.

We often group a merger and an acquisition together when we talk about this change for organizations and it's generally referred to as M&A. But they are different things. And each organization works through them differently. There is a need to be clear about which one you're dealing with and the way it is being handled. This is important because organizations are people and while it's easy to look at things on paper, you're dealing with people, egos and personalities, and that all needs to be considered. Quite often in an M&A process the levels of ambiguity are high. We know from Chapter 4 that this engenders fear and we know the impact that has on productivity.

Being mindful of what we have covered in this book already is so important as we apply the model to various situations.

A merger is usually a little softer in approach, with two parties coming together with complementary skill sets. An acquisition can be hostile. In fact, both can be hostile, depending on the reasons behind them happening in the first place. In an acquisition someone is acquiring someone else, so the consideration of the acquired organization is not as high as during a merger, in which the leadership and focus for the future are driven more by one party.

The challenge also comes around the business model of the acquiring organization. If they are an M&A growth business – they simply grow by acquiring smaller companies – then they should have a good process and plan in place to manage this. This is not always the case. I have seen many examples where organizations that grow through acquisition don't have a process around the people side of this. The communication with employees during the M&A is so important and when it comes to applying the Communication is often kept to a minimum until the M&A is complete. Sometimes there are legal reasons around this but it's important to have questions and answers ready as rumours will often fly around an organization.

There is a lot to be done during an M&A around due diligence, financial checking, conversations around future health, etc. It's a lot. So once the work is done and the deal is signed it can feel like a huge relief – but this is where it's just started for the people inside the organization. And if there is no communication, or a reliance on individuals to cascade, things can go wrong fast.

In both a merger and an acquisition, you will be:

- combining/resetting cultures;
- changing the business model;
- reviewing organizational design;
- potentially changing a brand as it is absorbed or a new one created;
- changing the operation of the organization.

Importantly, when you have identified that things aren't going well as a result of a merger or acquisition, there is a need to move fast. Sometimes the best intentions to bring people together have unintended damaging consequences as action is taken without time to diagnose and without listening. An important thing to watch out for is the closeness of leadership to the situation and the gap for employees. Often, leaders are so involved in the process they forget how much is unknown outside of that world.

Where things can go wrong:

- Creative campaign on values and brand done in isolation as a leadership team.
- No data gathered to understand how people feel.
- Lack of basics in place for those being acquired or merged into.
- Lack of transparency around process and timescales.
- No clear guiding principles from the [acquiring] company/ies on how to combine things.
- Lack of organizational strategy.
- Lack of people strategy.

It's not often the case that all of the problems listed happen at the same time. Quite often there is one or a few, but the impact of some of this is much deeper. The lack of basics in place for the companies involved make any next step challenging.

In some cases, none of these happen and the M&A will complete without any challenge, but it is rare. The ambiguity around how the two organizations work together often leads to confusion and when there is little focus on the operational impact, things get really difficult. At the start of this book I talked about the importance of understanding people and organizations. This is incredibly relevant for a merger/acquisition because a clear knowledge of both is needed to move forward.

Traditions of business focus purely on the financial impact and the financial relationship of the organizations but the human side is the most important. Organizations are people, so without considering them in the process is a huge risk to productivity and efficiency.

As you look to fix things longer term, this is where to start. Start with the foundations and to-do lists; you'll need a workshop with a mix of employees – probably several workshops over several days. The approach depends on the M&A strategy and inclusivity that is being given to the people involved but we can often forget that in going through an M&A, a new organization is being created.

Taking a people-first approach to the M&A and exploring what this looks like alongside the financials is the best way to start. If you're already in chaos after the M&A – go back and get those basics in place.

For the workshops and conversations, you'll need communications, HR and IT as the core departments to enable this to happen. People need information and they need to be listened to (communications). This is about people (HR) and they need to be connected to each other to work (IT). There will inevitably be others needed but let's start here, because involving too many people means you're in danger of decision by committee and working at a slower pace than what's needed.

The good news is that once you've built this foundation, it is much easier to continue with a strategy around M&A growth. It's also much easier to move forward because you're looking at and changing some of the most difficult aspects of an organization.

It is why purpose is so important and wraps around every aspect that exists for organizations, as discussed earlier in the book.

Table 8.2 outlines the diagnosis and themes linked to the process of an M&A once it is complete. The chaos is coming from combining organizations so the application of the model here is around the long-term future of the new organization that will exist.

Growing pains

Growth is always a tough one to manage through. And for smaller businesses, growth can happen quickly, which means there is a need to adapt to the change it brings. Businesses that start with a few people, grow to 20 people and then over 50 people over the course of years need to adapt processes and ways of working along the way. Catch this too late, and you've lost some good people who were with you from the start.

We talked about the impact of Covid-19 and the rhythm of organizations earlier in the book and it is here that we can refer back to those points. Growth requires a look at lots of aspects of the organization because small businesses are often reliant on simple conversations and informal networks, which diminish through growth.

For some leaders looking to grow, the chaos comes from a lack of knowing how to grow. Starting a business is daunting – you often don't know where the business is going to go and even if you have a plan, things can turn on a dime! Growth is exciting. Hiring people, exploring changes to the operation – they are all part of the leader's life and especially relevant for entrepreneurs. At this stage you are often working in the business a lot when there is a need to step out to work on the business. This is an important distinction to make. The role of the leader involves a lot of juggling. When there is growth on the agenda and you're a small team this makes for a lot of time working in the business.

Table 8.2 Fixing mergers and acquisitions using the Field Model

Understand the chaos	Diagnostic tool	Diagnostic themes to explore	The fix	Timescale – team size dependent
Combining/resetting cultures	Culture tracker and 1:1 conversations	Each individual culture and how it manifests, good and bad aspects of each for the future	Alignment against one set of values, behaviours, purpose co-created with employees	3–6 months
Changing the business model	1:1 interviews – predominantly leadership	What is the strategy, is the model aligned to that, are all models looking in the same direction?	Pivoting the organization to one purpose and creation of a clear strategic narrative	3–6 months
Reviewing organizational design	1:1 interviews and workshops to explore tasks	Does the organizational design support the business model and the culture?	Redesigning the organization for efficiency	3–12 months
Potentially changing a brand as it is absorbed or a new one created	1:1 interviews and brand workshop	What does the brand stand for today, does that align to the model and strategy? What is the value of the brand?	New brand in line with values and behaviours – this is the physical representation of the brand – name/logo, etc	3–6 months
Changing the operation of the organization	Surveys and 1:1 interviews	Underneath how things work in the separate organizations to map the crossover/duplication of work	Streamlined process and systems	6–18 months

Quite often, business owners are growing to sell and this can often be a focus at around five years in business, where there can be a desire to step back and let someone else take the reins. In most cases with smaller businesses, they haven't built something that can sustain that level of retraction. The business can be so reliant on the individual that stepping back isn't possible. If this is the plan, work needs to be done to enable that change in the time frame desired.

Growing doesn't have to be painful. Things that can slide in terms of teams or behaviours will be picked up through coaching and diagnosing the challenges. The ways of working can easily be challenged and changed with clarity of vision and working closely to enable a step forward.

This can be quick. Within two months the organization can be transformed, but it can also take years. It depends on the skills of the leader, the dynamics of the team, and the root cause of the pain and chaos that is being caused. As we look back on Chapter 1, we know that a strong strategic narrative is important for employee engagement. This is why the story of growth is so important to mitigate chaos.

For many leaders who are looking to explore why things are not working so well due to rapid growth, the symptoms they will see include:

- poor hiring choices;
- people off with stress;
- people not working well together hierarchically;
- lack of transparency of business performance;
- leaders not doing what they say they will.

In many cases these symptoms are easily addressed, and in organizations of fewer than 50 people things can turn at pace. But you have to catch this at the right time of growth. If you leave it too long without addressing the symptoms, it's harder to change.

When it comes to applying the model to growth chaos, the diagnostic tool will always be 1:1 interviews. This is because active listening is so important. When there has been a lot of growth the leadership team are often focused on that. People can feel left behind.

Table 8.3 Fixing growth challenges using the Field Model

Understand the chaos	Diagnostic tool	Diagnostic themes to explore	The fix	Timescale – team size dependent
Poor hiring choices	1:1 interviews	Process for hiring, onboarding, bias check, diversity and inclusion strategy	More robust processes for hiring that support the culture of the organization	1–2 months
People off with stress	1:1 interviews	The cause of the stress – workload, people, process	Find the themes that exist if there are several and workshop the issues/coaching for individuals	1–6 months
People not working well together hierarchically	1:1 interviews	The power struggle, parent-and-child relationships, task split	RASCI to support the ease of decision making and clear understanding of each other's needs/focus	2–12 months
Lack of transparency of business performance	1:1 interviews	What is stopping it? Lack of financial understanding, lack of strategic narrative	Create a way to tell the financial story that everyone is comfortable with	1–3 months
Leaders not doing what they say they will	1:1 interviews	Time management and productivity	Coaching	1–18 months

To ensure they don't feel that, a 1:1 interview means they are listened to. Someone is taking the time to really hear them and they can share any frustrations or concerns around every aspect of the organization. There might be a survey, depending on the size of the organization, but it's unlikely. This has to be a conversation about culture, communication, processes, leadership, trust and more.

The conversations are an agreed set of questions and the interviews should be around 45–90 minutes long, depending on how much people need to talk. We know the importance of listening and being present in those conversations will pay back hugely in terms of engagement.

In Table 8.3 you can see that when applied to problems of growth, the model produces different fixes from the other issues we have applied the model to. That's mainly because growth touches every aspect of the organization.

Global crisis

Crisis is a word often misused in organizations. Defining what is a crisis for your organization is often helpful and working with employees to define it can also be a great discussion, especially with front line/operational teams.

When a global crisis hits – like Covid-19 – the tools of the internal communicator will be some of the most important in the organization.

How does the Field Model work for a crisis?

The communications function will usually have a crisis plan in place. There is often a business continuity team and scenarios are often tested. Rachel Miller, Director of All Things IC, has a free guide on crisis communication, and it outlines the following steps:

- Team preparation – objectives, channels, accessibility, etc.
- Make links to external contacts – think about all stakeholders linked to the crisis.
- Announce and promote – make sure people know where to get information.

- Communicate and feedback as a crisis team.
- Monitor conversations from employees across channels – keep listening to adapt.
- Interact and respond to employees – if you have nothing to say it's OK to say that but you have to be part of the conversation.
- Always update and communicate – make sure your employee data is accurate.
- Practise and respond – this should be done in advance of a crisis – making sure you have a plan in place should it hit makes it easier to implement.
- Have a checklist so you know what to do when the crisis hits.

All of these are important and provide a good foundation for managing a crisis.

When it comes to applying the Field Model, in any crisis, it's about exploring things with a fresh perspective and a fresh view. A crisis can come in many forms and can vary in terms of impact. It can come from decisions made internally or it can be something external like Covid-19.

The Field Model is there to help you refocus the organization and review the cause and impact of the crisis. The impact of a crisis on every organization will be different. A global one will have huge impacts on all organizations but to varying degrees depending on so many factors.

We have talked about understand, diagnose and fix and for a global crisis, it looks something like Table 8.4.

In this sense a survey will work to get a snapshot of what is going on. In times of crisis, time is of the essence so interviews and focus groups won't be possible. While the survey might ask further questions, on analysis it will provide enough to enable steps forward.

Having a conversation with someone outside the organization helps achieve this and working through steps that break the normal working pattern will provide a different perspective on things.

A crisis will challenge an organization. The severity of the crisis will determine the action required. In 2020, the impact of Covid-19 was unprecedented and the need to look at the organization with a

Table 8.4   Using the Field Model in a global crisis

Understand	Diagnose	Fix (themes)
There has been a crisis and it has impacted the organization to the point of redundancies and a need to look at the organization in a different way to survive	You need data to understand more. Are there any aspects of the impact that have been compounded by internal processes or ways of working? Did the organization lose its way and is there a need to get back to the core of what it does? Is this a benefit? There might have been a need to change and this can be the catalyst to do it	Organizational design Processes that drive the organization – streamline/review Internal communication platforms to enable efficiency Skills training to be fit for the new skills or more urgent skills needed

fresh perspective was needed. The term 'pivot' became one of the most used words of the year, as organizations looked to adapt to the changes in market and consumer behaviour.

A crisis will heighten the good and the bad, in terms of both processes and behaviours. While there is a need to adapt and react swiftly, there is also a need to reflect on what worked before and what works now. Applying the model to a crisis means you are able to look at the symptoms that the crisis is highlighting.

If the crisis is self-made then you can explore all the fundamental aspects outlined throughout the book to explore why the crisis happened in the first place – it could be linked to leadership behaviours, processes, unethical decisions – it is a long list and a book in itself!

Some of the previous tables provide timescales that are quick. But in a crisis situation it has to be a more holistic view of the whole organization. It's easy if the crisis is very localized to a situation – like a collapsed supply chain that would impact the organization significantly. This requires a specific review of an existing process and is likely to lead to change in terms of provider or operation.

Larger-scale crisis – like the pandemic or a terrorist attack or something that impacts an entire community or organization – will have a longer lasting effect and require a different set of diagnostics to different timescales.

In both cases there might be a need to refocus the organization. To ensure that things are aligned to the purpose of the organization and that the activity to deliver against that purpose is the right activity. Internal communication will be at the core of doing this. We know that for leadership teams the focus of internal communication is heightened in a crisis. The panic and worry that hits employees thrusts it into the limelight for the CEO as the importance of getting information out to stakeholders becomes one of the most important tasks to keep things moving.

The important thing about a crisis is the powerful combination of leadership and communication that it encourages.

Fixing things from the top

We have discussed the importance of leadership throughout this book. The different types of leadership, the benefits of them and how it is important to find your own style and be genuine. When it comes to applying the Field Model for the long term we have to look at when chaos hits the leadership team.

We have looked at events that impact organizations as well as the chaos that can hit teams, but leadership as a group is another important one to consider. There has to be a consideration as to how that group works together and what symptoms can be seen when leadership isn't working well.

Whether you're a CEO or in a communications function, understanding the chaos that can come from leadership is important.

Earlier in the book I referenced Lencioni's five dysfunctions of a team, and these are specific to leadership:

- Absence of trust: The fear of being vulnerable with team members prevents the building of trust within teams.
- Fear of conflict: The desire to preserve artificial harmony stifles the occurrence of productive ideological conflict.

- Lack of commitment: The lack of clarity or buy-in prevents team members from making decisions they will stick to.
- Avoidance of accountability: The need to avoid interpersonal discomfort prevents team members from holding one another accountable.
- Inattention to results: The pursuit of individual goals and personal status erodes the focus on collective success.

Linked to some of these you can see the symptoms of chaos will suggest that the leadership and management of the organization needs to change:

- lack of alignment in the leadership team;
- inability to make decisions leading to lack of movement forward;
- lack of leadership skills;
- ego that stops progress.

To diagnose what is going on with leadership we need to focus on themes that are linked to the organization as well as to leaders as people – this is combining the theory known about organizations and people to reduce the chaos from the top. Table 8.5 explores how you can apply the Field Model to these symptoms to fix things at the top.

When it comes to exploring leadership and the organization from the top, I believe there are seven themes to explore: accountability, adaptability, capability, communication, connection, strategy and velocity:

1 **Accountability** – exploring how comfortable the team is with being accountable. This links to the ability to make decisions and manage the consequences. This isn't about blame and it's important to explore how people are held to account inside the organization.

2 **Adaptability** – how does the organization and the leadership team deal with change and failure?

3 **Capability** – does everyone have the right skills to do the job well? Does everyone have the right skills to do what's needed and if there are gaps, are they known and being acted upon? Importantly, do they have resource/capacity?

4 Communication – what does this look like for the organization? Are people clear? Is the communication effective? Do people have everything they need or want to know to do their jobs effectively? A desire to engage in conversation, not just one-way messaging. As the life blood of the organization this is a core component to explore.

5 Connection – an understanding of how connected teams are (in leadership) but also how connected the people are to the strategy and the purpose of the organization.

6 Strategy – checking to see if there is an understanding of what it is people should be working towards. Not just that they understand, but that they are undertaking activity that supports it.

7 Velocity – how the organization moves. How is it shaped and how quickly it can shift to respond to external forces.

Working through these themes with leaders, to diagnose what is going on, means you can work through a survey or 1:1 interviews – or both. They cover huge breadth in the organization looking at the impact of leadership on everything else.

Chapter 2 included a case study on Carillion, an organization that experienced challenges from the top. Had there been an awareness of the chaos around them and the need to address the symptoms that existed we have to wonder if the outcome for them could have been avoided. Applying this model and these seven themes to the leadership team should mean that the diagnosis covers enough aspects to fix things for the long term.

You can create questions that sit underneath the seven themes and link them to time. Are things how they should be now? Are they fit for the future? Asking the right questions for each theme will help you diagnose what is going on with the leadership team – just like the questions are important for the 1:1 listening interviews or other surveys that might be needed. Being mindful of bias and leading questions should always be top of mind as you look to fix things inside the organization.

Table 8.5 Using the Field Model with leadership teams

Understand the chaos	Diagnostic tool – team size dependent	Diagnostic themes to explore	The fix	Timescale – team size dependent
Lack of alignment in the leadership team	1:1 interviews or survey	Leadership team maturity – how long people have been in the role and how long the team has existed Any changes in direction/top team Legacy issues	Workshops and exploring Lencioni's five dysfunctions of a team Co-collaboration of a strategy and plan	6 months
Inability to make decisions leading to lack of movement forward	Employee insights – whatever method is used	Frustrated teams Lack of clarity from employees on how things get done Confused leadership team	RASCI Explore power with and power over dynamic in the leadership team	1–6 months
Lack of leadership skills	1:1 interviews or survey	Identify the skills needed – this is too broad to list	Development plans in place Coaching	2–12 months
Ego that stops progress	1:1 interviews	The power struggle, parent-and-child relationships, vulnerability and courage	Coaching	2–12 months

Fixing a toxic culture

One of the things we have covered in this book is the element of toxic chaos. This can link to a toxic culture. We have touched on the role of people as blockers and how that can cause chaos inside organizations too.

When there is a toxic culture it can manifest in these ways:

- disengaged employees;
- actively disengaged people, looking to bring others with them;
- blocking change.

For organizations where there are individuals actively against the strategy, the leadership team or the change that is coming, it can cause challenges for moving forward. I strongly believe that most people come to a situation with positive intent so that is why it's important to diagnose these things and find out what is going on underneath.

In some cases, it will be time for individuals to move on and in others, it can help shine a light on areas of focus for leadership and others in the team. What is important is that there is a conversation with honesty.

Actively disengaged people are often the biggest contributors to toxic cultures. If you're doing a survey and you ask about length of service, you can sometimes see a correlation to patterns of behaviour based on this. Sometimes this is because there is a cynicism around change, or 'it's not how it used to be' – what the data helps you identify is where the patterns are and whether length of service, or location, are triggers for the toxicity.

You'll notice in Table 8.6 that the timescales are incredibly broad for this. This is because there is a lot to uncover and a lot to manage. This is a strong people element and as a result, there needs to be consideration for the legalities around employment as well as the need for difficult conversations.

Sometimes people cannot be re-engaged. So when it comes to looking at the fix, this is the main question. If the answer is that they cannot be re-engaged then it is OK to part company. Our relationships with where we work can come to an end for all sorts of reasons. We find that ending incredibly challenging but like any relationship, you have to recognize when it is time to walk away, when it is no longer right for you.

Toxic cultures are linked so heavily to individual behaviours that they take time to unpick and understand. What feels toxic to one person might be totally OK for someone else so there is a lot to explore.

Here we have covered some specific people-related aspects but there is more that could be considered toxic culturally. A look at diversity and inclusion is always important as you examine what is impacting the culture in your organization.

Key points in this chapter

1 Applying the Field Model needs to bring all the chapters in this book together – internal communication, chaos, understanding people and organizations, diagnosing, understanding and fixing the problem.

2 The size of the organization or the team will determine how long things take to shift and the time investment required. This is often a journey of learning about the organization but also learning about yourself, and we all work at different speeds.

3 Understanding deskless workers and what makes a team is important. The research shows a difference between solitary, mixed and team workers and as such their communication needs are different.

4 There are different symptoms for different things that can impact organizations. How you diagnose those and fix them is also different but there are themes to look for in the diagnosis to enable the fix.

5 When fixing teams, be clear whether they are actually a team and what the fix is trying to achieve; explore why the team needs to work together, relationships and processes.

Table 8.6 Fixing toxic cultures with the Field Model

Understand the chaos	Diagnostic tool	Diagnostic themes to explore	The fix	Timescale – team size dependent
Disengaged employees	Survey and 1:1 interviews	The cause of the disengagement – bullying, value, manager, team	Can they be re-engaged or has it gone on for too long?	3 months – 2 years
Actively disengaged employees	1:1 interviews	Trust, explore what they want to achieve from the actions they are taking – what is their end goal?	Leaving the organization	3 months – 2 years
Blocking change	1:1 interviews	Get underneath the fear that is possibly driving the behaviours Speak to others to ensure the truth is coming through – sometimes they say one thing when others say something else	Moving into a different role, exploring the needs of the individual	3 months

6 There is a difference between a merger and an acquisition and this is an important distinction to make when applying the model as it's a different process with different outcomes culturally.

7 M&A fixes will explore cultures, processes, brands and the communication needed during the process.

8 Growth can bring different challenges around hiring choices, stress, organizational design and leadership integrity. In small businesses knowing how to grow and bring everyone with you can be an unknown skill.

9 Use a RASCI, coaching and explore processes to enable the growth to continue.

10 Remember that you need to consider the time to take people on the journey as well as going through the model. This is important as you help people understand what is happening and why.

11 A crisis inside an organization brings many challenges. Understand how to use the foundations of internal communication to manage it but apply the model to refocus the organization and identify where the crisis is coming from.

12 Organizations are people – they are the core component to enable things to happen so they shouldn't be forgotten, especially if you're in the conversations around a merger or acquisition.

13 Fixing things from the top requires a look at seven themes; accountability, adaptability, capability, communication, connection, strategy and velocity.

14 Looking at toxic culture and fixing it when there are actively disengaged people in the team can result in people leaving the organization. This is OK and we need to be comfortable that, just like any relationship, the work relationship can come to an end.

15 The challenge with a toxic culture is the long-term damage and the length of time it can take to manage the people involved. This can be anything from three months to two years and can have the biggest impact on organizational success.

Quick tips

- You need data to make decisions so invest time to diagnose what's happening.

- Remember that you need to take people on the journey of applying the model so they know what is happening.

- Use the right tool to gather data for the situation you're in and remember the tool you use says as much as the activity itself.

- Small things like fractured teams can have a broader impact on organizational success so don't ignore them until they become too big.

- Make sure you know the organizational strategy for growth or M&A – have conversations with the leadership team to help identify chaos before it happens!

References and further reading

Lencioni, P (2012) *The Five Dysfunctions of a Team: Facilitator's Guide: The official guide to conducting the five dysfunctions workshops for teams and team leaders*, Pfeiffer, San Francisco, CA

Miller, R (2020) Free crisis communication guide, All Things IC, www.allthingsic.com/free-crisis-communication-guide/ (archived at https://perma.cc/K5BU-MM5S)

Redefining Communications (2019) Remotely interested?, remotelyinterested.work/ (archived at https://perma.cc/BR7N-7J7U)

Conclusion

The steps to take to create influential internal communication

The Field Model has been designed to help anyone have an impact on the communication inside the organization. Not every company has an internal communication function so the purpose of this book is help anyone understand how to make a difference by following the steps to understand, diagnose and fix.

There is a fundamental need to better understand each other to make organizations successful for the longer term. The impact of Covid-19 and the change to work has heightened this need. With workforces scattered in different locations and hybrid working from different locations becoming the norm, the need for communication to be better inside organizations can't be ignored.

A better understanding of people – our need for certainty, less ambiguity and how we respond to fear all help us navigate the world of work. We spend one-third of our time there yet we seem to invest so little in it as a place to provide care and consideration for others. This isn't always the case and there are case studies from organizations who are doing brilliant work in communicating internally but the data and insight over the last 10 years alone tells us it is not enough.

Organizations are going to change again. We have touched on the role of globalization and the role technology has played to date but there are further spikes coming from the roll-out of AI and the need for teams to adapt on the back of Covid-19.

In 2020, Netflix released their exclusive documentary-drama *The Social Dilemma*, which addressed the fears and concerns people have around the huge surge in the use of social networks. During the documentary, Randima (Randy) Fernando, co-founder of the Center for Humane Technology, comments on the challenges the pace of technology brings to the human race:

> From the 1960s to today, processing power has gone up about a trillion times. Nothing else that we have has improved at anything near that rate. Cars are roughly twice as fast and almost everything else is negligible. And perhaps most importantly, our human – our physiology, our brains, have evolved not at all.

Our brains are the fundamental thing that is important in us as people, because while the world around us continues to change and innovate with technology and pace, our brains are much the same as they were millions of years ago. Our instincts are the same, our gut reactions are the same and our reasons for fear and trust the same.

If we don't take the time to understand this then communication is difficult. We are social animals who need social connection and that connection comes from relationships, which in turn come from communication.

The Field Model codifies the process for influential internal communication. The major step in the process is diagnosing what is going on and shifting us away from treating the symptoms of poor communication and poor relationships.

We cannot continue to run organizations without this investment. We have to look deeper into the role of profit and purpose and the impact it has on the people who do all the work for you.

The biggest investment we can give is time. The fix does not have to have a financial impact on the organization. It's about refocusing efforts on the things that we can take for granted. The things we assume and ignore that lead to toxicity. Having the courage to address those and explore them will lead to better communication and in turn, better relationships. Giving ourselves the skills and framework to do that is what the Field Model is for.

There is a lot covered in this book, so in this concluding chapter I want to outline clear steps to take to enable you to achieve influential internal communication.

1 Your own skills and continuous learning

It's important that we invest in ourselves. As leaders or communicators we need to make sure we are continuously learning and adapting to the changing world of work. In relation to internal communication, and the reason there is such a focus on being human, there has to be a focus on understanding each other more. The model in this book provides you with a framework to help you move forward. Underpinned by research and industry reports, there is a clear method you can follow – and a clearer understanding of the importance of people and, in turn, yourself.

The profession map from the IoIC in Chapter 1 is also something to draw on – make sure you're equipped to make the changes your organization needs.

2 Understand the symptoms

The first step in the Field Model is to understand what is going on. You need to ask questions, be curious. To understand the symptoms, you'll need to have visibility of some of the key organizational objectives or key performance indicators. Often this includes employee retention and this will show you if there is an issue in this area to explore. Conversations with leaders might tell you there are issues with teams, toxic cultures or plans for growth – all of these conversations will help you understand what's happening in the organization and if there is any risk of chaos.

3 Diagnose what's going on

We have talked in depth about data and diagnostic tools. Chapter 6 outlines details of the different ways you can do this and the best methods for different situations. This is also the foundation of the internal communication model outlined in Chapter 1 – insight. Without it we cannot know for sure what is happening. Combining surveys with listening interviews is a great combination to uncover how people feel, how they know things and what's really happening. The conversations here require you to ask questions and create an environment where people feel safe to share.

This doesn't have to take months, either. Sometimes the thing that stops us doing this is the worry of how long it will take. The fear that it will take so long, making it feel like an unachievable task. This isn't the case and it can be done in a matter of weeks.

4 Analyse the findings and explore them alongside the business intelligence

There has to be analysis of the findings. The review of the survey data, the conversations and what they tell you. This should also include a look at business intelligence, which is the second part of the model outlined in Chapter 1. The intelligence should tell you more about the channels that exist in the organization, the content that is shared, the leadership style, the culture and more. You will have a huge amount of insight here and it's important to take the time to review it and make sense of it. This is a good exercise to do with others in the team, to work through and ensure there is no bias coming into the analysis.

Grouping things into themes, like we did in Chapter 7 where we talked about the fix, enables you to see how you can solve the issues thematically.

5 The conversations to enable the fix

Once the analysis is complete and the report created, the conversations with leadership have to take place. Often this is a 1:1 with the CEO or MD, followed by a conversation with the broader leadership team. In some cases, some other members of the board will want a 1:1 to explore anything specific for them to work on too – this is gold dust! I am delighted when this happens as I know that the individuals are in the right, evolutionary mindset to enable the change.

Make sure this conversation takes place in a safe place and that enough time is allowed. It shouldn't be a formal presentation – it has to be a discussion.

At this stage you can agree what is going to happen. There is likely to be a list of things in the fix report with key actions under the themes. Working through this list, prioritizing items and working out the quick wins and the long-term focus is important, as it enables a plan to be created to work through.

6 Tell the story

Make sure you're taking the time here to share the story with employees – tell them what's happening as a result of the insight gathering and diagnosis. This is important and should also include elements of what was covered in Chapter 4. Helping employees understand more about themselves and why they feel the way they do helps everyone feel more comfortable with change. When I share the story with the teams and explain that the way they feel about the ambiguity they are in is normal, I can see a physical response to knowing they are not alone.

Use this time to enable connections between teams and each other, and start with the intention of making things more human.

7 The fix itself

We know that the fix itself can take anything from a few months to a few years. A lot depends on the people, the budget and the focus for the organization. What is important in the fix is a time frame. We don't need constant change – that is chaos. We need small projects that can be managed to completion – like creating an employee induction, job descriptions, a new process for sales, new templates for sales calls – there could be hundreds! But each one can have a timescale and a completion date.

You're taking things from chaos to calm by helping people communicate better inside the organization. Upskilling them will also be on the list and should be done at the start of the overall fix.

8 Measuring success

You will want to measure the success of the changes. This isn't about measuring the level of calm but it is about ensuring the changes are having a business impact. You should be able to see real change to enable an organization to move forward. You can go deeper and measure it with a financial impact in terms of sales and staff retention too. What's important is that this is aligned to the symptoms you have identified and the KPIs that were uncovered.

These eight steps combine the thinking throughout this book. The detail to support you in fixing the organization is in Chapter 8 where tables outline specific ways to remove the chaos in different circumstances.

There is a lot to do in organizations today to enable influential internal communication, but it doesn't need to take huge amounts of time. Things can be broken down into bite-size chunks, focused into 30-, 60- and 90-day plans, and action can be taken to make a difference.

The Field Model has been created to enable you to take small steps forward. Working through the symptoms and recognizing how they impact your organization. By reading this book you are taking the first steps to find the calm in the chaos. Diagnosing it, working through how to change it together takes time. The fixes that will be identified can be worked through step by step. This isn't a quick fix. It was never intended to be one. Organizations are people. Changing behaviours, taking people on a journey and making time for the right things to take the organization forward takes courage – but it will bring calm.

References and further reading

Orlowski, J (dir.) (2020) *The Social Dilemma*, Netflix [film]

Redefining Communications (nd) How we can help, redefiningcomms.com/
what-we-do/ (archived at https://perma.cc/GPL3-RBZ5)

INDEX

CPSIA information can be obtained
at www.ICGtesting.com
Printed in the USA
LVHW071656171122
733427LV00005B/184